GW01396217

ASIA
Express

For Mum and Dad, who showed me the world.
And for Tim, who gave me the world.

ASIA
Express

100 FAST & EASY FAVOURITES

MARION GRASBY

plum. Pan Macmillan Australia

CONTENTS

INTRODUCTION
PAGE 007

IN THE PANTRY
PAGE 010

WOK TIPS
PAGE 015

SEAFOOD
PAGE 017

BEEF & LAMB
PAGE 123

VEGGIES & EGGS
PAGE 149

CHICKEN & DUCK
PAGE 057

PORK
PAGE 095

RICE
PAGE 177

SWEET THINGS & DRINKS
PAGE 191

WEEKLY DINNER PLANNER
PAGE 210

COOKING FOR FRIENDS
PAGE 212

THANKS
PAGE 217

INDEX
PAGE 218

HELLO

It's no secret that food is one of the great loves of my life – I'm utterly, hopelessly enthralled by all things tasty. I love nothing more than a lazy Saturday spent pottering around making fresh, pungent curry pastes or rolling out whispy strands of egg noodles. The problem is that lazy Saturdays don't seem to come around that often, let alone lazy Mondays, Tuesdays or any day of the week for that matter. Most days I find myself with no more than half an hour to get dinner on the table but I still want to feel inspired, creative and, most importantly, happy to share the love with family and friends at my table. And I know a lot of you feel the same way.

Many of you have written to tell me your stories – how much your family loves a quick Thai green curry after football training or that your three-year-old tried fried rice for the first time and loved every messy handful that made it into her mouth. It's your stories that have encouraged me to write this book. Simple, fast and inspired recipes for busy lives are what *Asia Express* is all about.

And the good news is that it's so very easy to create quick, brilliant Asian dishes at home. Each recipe in this book should take you no longer than 30 minutes. These are the recipes I come back to, time and time again. They are my treasured possessions, collected during a childhood spent in my mother's kitchen and through a lifetime of travelling and living in Asia.

Inspiration

Growing up with a Thai mother meant my love for Asian food was inevitable. I take comfort in the fragrant smell of a Thai curry, the smoky char from a well-used wok, or the eye-watering sting from stir-fried chillies. All these things speak to me of home, my family and the places I love. Asian flavours inspire my everyday meals, no matter how little time I have to cook.

The recipes in this book are flavoured by the many Asian countries and cuisines I've fallen in love with. You'll find recipes from Thailand, Japan, Malaysia, Singapore, India, Vietnam, Burma, China and Korea. I'm a devoted food traveller. New recipes, flavours and ingredients mean far more to me than any souvenir shop trinkets. I can remember with distinct clarity every savoury, spring onion-packed bite of the Korean pancakes I ate in a market shop in Seoul. At a tiny hole-in-the-wall restaurant in Shanghai my tastebuds literally tingled with excitement as I devoured a stir-fry laden with fiery chillies and Sichuan peppercorns. Even Bangkok traffic isn't enough to stop me getting to my favourite noodle soup cart on the other side of town. And now I can share these treasured finds and flavours with you.

How to use this book

A well-stocked pantry makes my life much simpler, so I've given you a list of my essential ingredients with 'In the Pantry' (page 10). Use this as a guide for ingredients you may want to pick up during your regular grocery shop; where a special trip to an Asian grocer is required I've tried to make it worth your while by including those items in multiple recipes.

I've divided the recipes into proteins; vegetables and eggs; rice; and sweet things and drinks. There are things to snack on, things to drink and meals to make. I've given suggestions for sides or complementary recipes. You will know best what you and your family like to eat, so feel free to create your own combinations. There are no rules!

Keeping it simple

Every time I visit my family in their rural Thai village I'm reminded of how very few bits and bobs are needed to cook beautiful food. My grandma and aunties do most of their cooking outdoors using a charcoal brazier and a single wok. From their simple 'kitchen' under a big shady tree come comforting rice soups, fiery stir-fries and amazing spicy curries. These wise ladies are my true food heroes.

So a simple kitchen is all you'll need to work your way through the recipes in this book. Apart from the usual chopping and frying implements, the other special piece of equipment I find necessary in my kitchen is a good, solid mortar and pestle for grinding spices and making pastes. I also like to keep a small, handheld food processor on hand to make light work of finely chopping ingredients. And of course I couldn't live without my trusty wok (see more on woks later on page 15).

So here's to the tasty times ahead. I hope you find some new friends within these pages. These are the recipes I love to use every day and I hope they find a place in your home too.

I'd love to hear from you, so drop me a line at:
www.facebook.com/mariongrasby
www.marionskitchen.com.au

Keep it tasty!

LOVE,
MARION

IN THE PANTRY

Here is a list of my favourite things – my secret bag of tricks, if you like. Rather than a comprehensive glossary of Asian ingredients likely to sit gathering dust in a bottom drawer, these are the pantry items that I use time and time again. Each ingredient is used multiple times throughout this book and you'll find suggestions below each on how to make even more use of them.

BAMBOO SHOOTS

These are the edible new shoots of the bamboo plant. The shoots themselves don't have bags of flavour but when added to dishes they act like little sponges and soak up any tasty sauces. They're mainly sold pre-sliced in cans. To use, drain and discard the brine they come in and add the shoots to stir-fries, curries or soups.

DRIED SHRIMP

In Asian cooking, dried shrimp are used more as a seasoning ingredient than a substitute for fresh prawns. They're mildly fishy and quite salty and add a savoury, umami quality to any dish. Once opened, keep them in your refrigerator for up to a month. Try tossing a small handful into wok-fried Asian greens or stir-fried noodles.

FRIED SHALLOTS/ ONIONS

Packets of ready-made fried onions or shallots can be bought from the Asian aisle of most supermarkets or an Asian grocer. You can also make your own by finely slicing shallots and deep-frying them in hot oil. WARNING: they are very addictive! Sprinkle them over salads, rice or mashed potatoes for an added toasty crunch.

CHINESE BLACK VINEGAR

This dark rice vinegar has a complexity of flavour more similar to a young balsamic than regular varieties of white or red wine vinegars. It has a mellow acidic quality that is balanced with a little fruitiness and a hint of smokiness. Try adding a splash to sauces, stir-fries, marinades and soups.

FISH SAUCE

There are loads of different fish sauces available, with many brands from Thailand and Vietnam. With my Thai heritage I'm a little biased towards the former. Whichever one you go for, think of your fish sauce as an essential seasoning that emphasises flavours in a similar way to salt.

Add a few splashes as a quick marinade for meat or seafood before stir-frying. Or make a quick dipping sauce by mixing it with some finely sliced chillies and a squeeze of lime juice.

GARAM MASALA

A big hit of Indian spices ready to go in one handy packet, garam masala is a blend of spices — usually pepper, cloves, cinnamon, cumin seeds and cardamom. Simply mixed with a little oil and salt, it makes a super marinade for prawns, steak or chicken.

GOCHUJANG (KOREAN CHILLI PASTE)

This pungent chilli paste is made from red chillies, rice and fermented soy beans. It has a deep, dark-red colour and a slightly smoky flavour. Add a spoonful to your next stir-fry or mix it with mayonnaise for a simple sandwich spread. You can find it in rectangular tubs, usually red-coloured, at most Asian grocers. At a pinch you can sometimes substitute sriracha chilli sauce and I've indicated where that's possible in the recipes in this book.

'KEWPIE' (JAPANESE) MAYONNAISE

Japanese-style mayonnaise usually comes in the squishy cream-coloured bottle you might have seen in the Asian section of your local supermarket. 'Kewpie' is a popular brand. It's tangy, sweet and oh-so-delicious in sandwiches and as a dipping sauce for all manner of things. Try mixing it with wasabi or a little hot chilli sauce for a spicy kick.

PALM SUGAR

Palm sugar is extracted from the sap of palm trees. It varies in colour from light golden tan to dark brown. It is generally sold in block form, so you need to shave off slices with a knife. Palm sugar has a deep caramel-like taste, similar to a light molasses or treacle. Use it to add a little sweetness to Thai curries or try using it instead of white sugar to make caramel. Find it in the Asian section of major supermarkets or from an Asian grocer.

OYSTER SAUCE

I like to call this 'magic sauce'. It's a thick, salty and slightly sweet sauce that ramps up the flavour of any stir-fry, marinade or Asian soup. Try mixing it with a little water to thin it down to drizzling consistency and then simply pour over steamed Asian greens.

PANKO BREADCRUMBS

These Japanese-style breadcrumbs are light, fluffy and incredibly crisp. Try them with any recipe that calls for breadcrumbs.

SAMBAL OELEK

This hot chilli paste, sold in jars and available from the Asian aisle of most supermarkets and found in every Asian grocer, is a good alternative to fresh chillies. Use it to add spice to soups and salads, or as a spicy condiment for grilled chicken or pork.

SESAME OIL

Flavour bomb in a bottle! Sesame oil has a nutty toastiness that adds a unique flavour to stir-fries, sauces or marinades. Mix with a little soy sauce, a dash of Chinese black vinegar and chilli powder for an easy dumpling dipping sauce. Find it in the Asian aisle of most supermarkets or from any Asian grocer.

SHAOXING (CHINESE COOKING WINE)

Shaoxing is a Chinese wine made from fermented rice. Use it to add flavour to Asian broths, stocks and stir-fries.

SHICHIMI TOGARASHI

Also known as 'Japanese seven-spice', this is a blend of tasty treats, most commonly chilli, citrus peel, sesame seeds, ginger and nori. Use it as an all-purpose, tangy chilli sprinkle – on potatoes, fried chicken, tempura prawns, battered fish, salted peanuts … the list could go on forever.

SHIRO MISO

Also known as 'white' or 'sweet' miso, shiro miso is not as salty as the darker varieties of miso and has a lovely, delicate, savoury flavour. Add it to your mashed potatoes for a big umami kick.

SRIRACHA CHILLI SAUCE

This is a type of hot sauce thought to be named after the region of Si Racha in Thailand, where it is believed to have originated. Sriracha chilli sauce is packed with chilli spice and quite tangy. It is also sold simply as 'Hot Chilli Sauce' in the Asian section of most supermarkets. It's great as a dipping sauce for grilled chicken or try mixing it through mayonnaise for a kick-ass, all-purpose, spicy sauce.

SHRIMP PASTE

Made from ground, fermented shrimp, I call this the Vegemite of Asian cooking because of its pungent, full-on smell. It has a very strong, salty and fishy flavour on its own but once added to dishes it seems to mellow out and supply a background umami flavour. Some major supermarkets stock shrimp paste in their Asian aisle or you can find it at any Asian grocer.

SICHUAN PEPPERCORNS

Wow, these really pack a punch. Sichuan peppercorns have a citrus-like aroma and create a tingly, numbing sensation on your tongue – seriously addictive. Make a Sichuan salt for sprinkling over noodles or roasted meats – simply toast a spoonful in a dry frying pan before using a mortar and pestle to grind it with some sea salt.

SOY SAUCE

While less is often more when it comes to soy sauce, I advocate buying at least two or possibly three different types. Using the right soy sauce for different dishes will make a big difference to the flavour and colour of your cooking.

Dark soy sauce adds a rich, deep colour; it has a strong molasses flavour and is less salty than light soy sauce. I use light soy sauce as a general, all-purpose seasoning as it has a savoury, salty flavour, but without the dark colour. Most Chinese recipes that specify 'soy sauce' are actually referring to light soy sauce.

Japanese soy sauce has a slightly sweeter, more mellow flavour than light soy sauce but a stronger, darker colour. A popular brand is Kikkoman. Most major supermarkets stock light and Japanese soy sauces. Dark soy sauce can be a little more difficult to find so you may have to take a trip to your Asian grocer for that one.

TONKATSU SAUCE

This Japanese-style barbecue sauce is typically served with crumbed pork cutlets. I use it wherever I would use a regular barbecue sauce. It's an excellent sauce for grilled sausages!

WOK TIPS

You will get to know the inside of a wok very well as you work your way through the recipes in this book. Of course if you don't have a wok you could use a large, deep frying pan for any stir-fried dish but I find wok cooking is a magical process. The heat, movement and what's called 'the breath of the wok' gives stir-fried food that characteristic smoky, charry flavour.

There's no need to spend a fortune on some fancy-pants type of wok. I find the thin carbon steel woks you find at most Asian grocers are all you need – they're inexpensive and they heat up quickly and evenly.

A non-stick surface is great if you're not too confident. My preference, though, is for a non-coated carbon steel wok with a flat bottom that makes it easier to keep it from sliding around too much. And woks respond best to naked flame. But if you don't have a gas stove you could also use those portable gas camping stoves that come pretty cheap at hardware stores.

....

SEASONING A WOK

If you go with an uncoated carbon steel number then you'll need to 'season' your wok to keep it from rusting, but also to develop that characteristic 'breath of the wok' flavour. Here's how to do it …

STEP 1
Wash and scrub the inside of the wok thoroughly in soapy water to remove any factory oil. Place it over a high flame to dry out.

STEP 2
Remove from the heat and pour in a couple of tablespoons of vegetable oil. Use kitchen paper to rub the inside of the wok with the oil.

STEP 3
Place your wok back over high heat. Now move the wok around so that the bottom and edges heat up and change colour. Your wok should start to become dark and burnished from the centre up to the edges. Now you're ready to go!

....

To care for your seasoned wok, wash it with water after each use (soap can damage your hard-earned seasoning) and use a wok brush to gently scrub any stubborn bits.

SEAFOOD

01. PRAWN CAKES WITH CHILLI–LIME SAUCE — 018
02. CRISPY FISH WITH CHILLI SAMBAL — 020
03. WOK-FRIED PRAWNS — 023
04. VIETNAMESE TURMERIC & DILL FISH — 024
05. SPICED ROASTED SALMON — 026
06. PRAWN CHAR KWAY TEOW — 028
07. SESAME TUNA WITH PONZU — 031

FISH PARCELS 3 WAYS
08. SWEET CHILLI & LIME PARCELS — 033
09. CORIANDER & GARLIC PARCELS — 034
10. SOY & GINGER PARCELS — 034

11. CRAB OMELETTE — 036
12. GRILLED LOBSTER WITH KAFFIR LIME BUTTER — 039
13. THAI RED CURRY–POACHED SALMON — 040
14. BURMESE PRAWN CURRY — 041
16. CRUMBED CORIANDER FISH FINGERS — 042
17. THAI YELLOW CURRY CRAB — 045
18. KOREAN SEAFOOD PANCAKES — 046
19. VIETNAMESE PRAWN SALAD — 048
20. THAI GREEN SEAFOOD CURRY — 050
21. PRAWN MEE GORENG — 051
22. SOUTH INDIAN FISH CURRY — 053
23. SLIGHTLY CHARRY CHAR SIU SALMON — 054

PRAWN CAKES WITH CHILLI–LIME SAUCE

MAKES ABOUT 25, READY IN 30 MINUTES

600 g peeled and deveined raw
   prawns (about 1.2 kg if you're
   buying them unpeeled)
1 garlic clove, finely chopped
¼ cup finely sliced spring onions
¼ cup roughly chopped fresh
   coriander
¼ cup mint leaves
5 kaffir lime leaves, central
   stems removed and leaves
   finely sliced
1 egg white
1 teaspoon sea salt
½ teaspoon ground black pepper
vegetable oil for deep-frying

Chilli–lime sauce
¼ cup sweet chilli sauce
1 tablespoon lime juice
1 teaspoon fish sauce

I use the 'pinch and fry' method for my prawn cakes because it seems a whole lot quicker than fiddling around with shaping perfectly round little patties and laying them out on a tray. I quite like the odd-shaped morsels this method produces. If you're making them in advance for a party, by all means shape your prawn cakes early and set them out on a tray lined with plastic wrap.

They also freeze well – just place them in the freezer on the tray covered with plastic wrap and, once they're frozen, transfer them to zip-lock bags to save space. You can cook them from frozen.

STEP 1
Preheat the oven to 150°C.

STEP 2
To make the chilli–lime sauce, mix the ingredients in a small bowl and set aside until ready to serve.

STEP 3
Place the prawns, garlic, spring onions, coriander, mint, kaffir lime leaves, egg white, salt and black pepper in the bowl of a food processor and pulse until you have a smooth paste. Scoop the sticky mixture out into a large bowl.

STEP 4
Fill a wok one-third full with vegetable oil and heat to 180°C. If you don't have a cooking thermometer, a cube of bread will turn golden in 30 seconds when the oil is hot enough.

STEP 5
Wet your hands with water and pinch off small bits (about a tablespoon at a time) of the prawn mixture and carefully drop them into the hot oil. Don't overcrowd your wok – about eight at a time should do. Cook for 2–3 minutes, then remove the prawn cakes and drain on paper towel. Keep them warm in the preheated oven. Repeat this process until you have used all the prawn mixture.

STEP 6
Serve the prawn cakes with chilli–lime sauce.

CRISPY FISH WITH CHILLI SAMBAL

SERVES 4, READY IN 20 MINUTES

vegetable oil for shallow-frying

4 × 200 g snapper fillets, skin on
(or any other fish fillets
you fancy)

sea salt

¼ cup plain flour

2 spring onions, trimmed
and finely sliced into long,
whispy strands

Chilli sambal

3 eschallots, roughly chopped

4 garlic cloves, roughly chopped

2 long red chillies, roughly
chopped

3 tablespoons vegetable oil

2 tomatoes, chopped

2 tablespoons fish sauce

2 tablespoons tamarind
concentrate

3 tablespoons honey

This chilli sambal is one of my 'keeper' recipes I have filed away for all sorts of uses. Serve it with grilled prawns or scallops, or use as a dipping sauce for spring rolls.

You can serve your fish Asian-style with plain or fried rice (see pages 178, 181 and 182 for recipes). I also like to dish it up with mashed potatoes or a lovely crisp green salad.

STEP 1

Begin by making the chilli sambal. Combine the eschallots, garlic and chillies in a food processor and pulse until finely chopped (you could also do this by hand).

STEP 2

Heat the vegetable oil in a small saucepan over medium–high heat and cook the eschallot mixture until soft (about 5 minutes). Add the tomatoes, fish sauce, tamarind concentrate and honey and simmer for 10 minutes, until the tomatoes break down and the sauce thickens.

STEP 3

While the sambal is cooking, pour the vegetable oil into a large non-stick frying pan to a depth of 1 cm. Place over medium–high heat. Season the fish fillets with salt, then lightly coat with flour. Fry the fish fillets in oil for 3–4 minutes on each side, until cooked through. Drain on paper towel.

STEP 4

Spoon a generous amount of chilli sambal onto the serving plates. Top with the fish fillets and spring onions.

WOK-FRIED PRAWNS

12 raw jumbo tiger prawns,
  peeled (with heads and tails
  intact) and deveined
lime wedges to serve

Marinade
3 garlic cloves, finely chopped
1 long red chilli, finely chopped
3 kaffir lime leaves, stems
  removed, very finely sliced
finely grated zest of 1 lime
2 tablespoons lime juice
2 tablespoons fish sauce
3 tablespoons vegetable oil
½ teaspoon white sugar

The easiest way to get fine strands of kaffir lime leaves is to rip out the centre stem from each leaf, pile the leaves on top of each other, and roll them up tightly into a cigar shape. Now take your knife and finely shave off teeny, tiny little strands.

You could serve these on their own as an entrée for a dinner or lunch party or as part of an Asian banquet–style meal.

STEP 1
To make the marinade, place the ingredients in a large bowl and mix thoroughly.

STEP 2
Add the prawns and toss to coat in the mixture. Set aside to marinate for 10 minutes.

STEP 3
Heat a wok over high heat. When the wok is smoking hot, add the prawns and the marinade and stir-fry for 2 minutes, until the prawns start to change colour. Add ¼ cup of water and stir-fry for another 2–3 minutes, or until the prawns are just cooked through.

STEP 4
Serve with lime wedges.

VIETNAMESE TURMERIC & DILL FISH

SERVES 4, READY IN 20 MINUTES

4 × 200 g white fish fillets, sliced into strips about 4 cm wide

180 g dried rice vermicelli noodles

2 tablespoons vegetable oil

2 tablespoons lime juice

1 long red chilli, finely sliced

Marinade

⅓ cup sliced spring onions (white and green parts)

3 garlic cloves, roughly chopped

¼ cup fish sauce

1 tablespoon turmeric

2 teaspoons curry powder

2 teaspoons white sugar

2 tablespoons vegetable oil

¼ cup finely chopped fresh dill

In a tiny hole-in-the-wall restaurant in Hanoi I fell in love with an intoxicating fish dish called *'cha ca'*. Sizzling fish is laced with dill, turmeric and curry powder and served with vermicelli noodles to mop up the rich, savoury sauce.

STEP 1

For the marinade, use a mortar and pestle to pound the spring onion and garlic to a rough paste. Stir through the remaining marinade ingredients. Pour the marinade into large bowl, add the fish and toss to coat.

STEP 2

Cook the vermicelli noodles in boiling water for 2 minutes, until tender. Drain and rinse under running water to cool. Use scissors to roughly cut the noodles into shorter lengths. Divide between the four serving bowls.

STEP 3

Heat the vegetable oil in a large non-stick frying pan over medium–high heat and cook the fish for 2 minutes on one side, or until golden brown. Turn the fish over and add ½ cup of water. Cover with a lid and simmer for 2–3 minutes, or until the fish is just cooked. Pour over the lime juice and remove from the heat.

STEP 4

To serve, top the noodles with the fish and sauce, and garnish with red chilli slices.

SPICED ROASTED SALMON

1 side salmon (about 1.5 kg),
  skinned and pin-boned
2 tablespoons vegetable oil
2 teaspoons ground coriander
2 teaspoons ground cumin
2 teaspoons paprika
¼ teaspoon turmeric
1 teaspoon sea salt
fresh coriander to serve
mint leaves to serve

Mint and coriander yoghurt
1 cup roughly chopped fresh
  coriander
½ cup mint leaves
1 small garlic clove
2 tablespoons lemon juice
¾ cup thick natural yoghurt

A whole side of roasted salmon is such an easy way to feed a large family or dinner party guests. Instead of fiddling around cooking individual portions of salmon, the whole thing goes into the oven and is then served as it is. Perfectly easy and perfectly tasty. A green salad, mashed potatoes, roasted potatoes or my Spiced Indian Rice (page 184) are great side dishes for this salmon.

STEP 1

Preheat the oven to 200°C.

STEP 2

Lay the salmon on a large baking tray lined with foil. In a small bowl, mix the vegetable oil, coriander, cumin, paprika, turmeric and salt to make a spicy paste. Spread the paste over the top of the salmon. Roast the salmon in the oven for 18–20 minutes, or until just cooked through. When cooked, the salmon should flake easily when prodded with a fork.

STEP 3

While the salmon is cooking, make the mint and coriander yoghurt. Place the ingredients in the bowl of a food processor and whizz until smooth. Transfer to a small bowl.

STEP 4

To serve, transfer the salmon to a large platter (or to make it even easier, you can just leave it on the baking tray you roasted it on). Scatter with fresh coriander and mint leaves and serve with the yoghurt on the side.

PRAWN CHAR KWAY TEOW

2 tablespoons vegetable oil

3 garlic cloves, finely chopped

1 Chinese sausage (lap cheong),*
sliced on the diagonal

200 g peeled and deveined raw
prawns (about 400 g if you're
buying them unpeeled)

1 egg, lightly whisked

300 g fresh rice noodles,*
cut into strips about 2 cm wide

½ cup spring onions, cut into
3 cm batons

chilli flakes to serve

Stir-fry sauce

3 tablespoons light soy sauce

1 tablespoon dark soy sauce

2 teaspoons Chinese black
vinegar*

1 teaspoon white sugar

A good wok-fry will impart a smoky, charry flavour from what's called the 'breath of the wok'. My biggest tip for achieving that 'breath' or slight smokiness is to heat your wok to the point where you're a little bit scared. The oil in your wok should be so hot that it's just starting to tremble and release little tendrils of smoke. In other words, it should be scary hot!

Have everything chopped and ready to go before that first ingredient hits the pan because the whole process needs to be super fast. When you add your ingredients they should sizzle, smoke and char straight away. If you plan to increase the quantities for this recipe to serve more than two people, I suggest making it in batches so that you can keep up that super hot wok temperature throughout the cooking.

STEP 1
Whisk the sauce ingredients together until well combined and set aside until ready to use.

STEP 2
Heat the vegetable oil in a wok over high heat. Add the garlic and Chinese sausage and stir-fry for 1 minute.

STEP 3
Now add the prawns and cook for 1–2 minutes, or until just cooked. Move everything to one side of the wok and pour the lightly whisked egg into the empty side. Let the egg set for 30 seconds or so, flicking the raw egg from the centre to the outer edges to help it cook evenly. Break up the egg with a spatula and toss everything together.

STEP 4
Add the noodles and the sauce and cook, tossing everything around, for another minute or so. Remove from the heat and toss through the spring onions. Serve with chilli flakes to taste.

* Chinese sausages (lap cheong) are available in the Asian section of most major supermarkets or from Asian grocers.

* Fresh rice noodles are available at Asian grocers. If you're using them straight from the fridge they'll be stiff, so nuke them in the microwave for 30 seconds to soften before using.

* Chinese black vinegar is a dark, complex vinegar that you can find at your Asian grocer.

SESAME TUNA WITH PONZU

4 × 180 g tuna steaks
sea salt
½ cup sesame seeds (a mixture
  of black and white seeds
  is nice)
vegetable oil for shallow-frying

Ponzu
1 tablespoon finely sliced
  spring onion
2 tablespoons Japanese soy
  sauce
1 tablespoon rice vinegar
finely grated zest of 1 lemon
2 tablespoons lemon juice
1 tablespoon honey
1 teaspoon wasabi paste
1 teaspoon finely grated
  fresh ginger

Home-made ponzu sauce has such a distinctive, fresh, citrussy flavour. I adore it on just about anything – tuna, salmon, ocean trout, seared steaks, even on steamed green vegetables. Wok-fried bok choy, rice or mashed potato make great sides for this dish.

STEP 1
Whisk together the ingredients for the ponzu and set aside until ready to serve.

STEP 2
Sprinkle the tuna with salt and coat in sesame seeds.

STEP 3
Heat enough oil to just coat the base of a large non-stick frying pan and place over medium–high heat. Cook the tuna for 2 minutes on each side (for rare), or longer if you like it well cooked.

STEP 4
Serve the tuna steaks whole or cut into thick slices, and drizzled with ponzu.

FISH PARCELS

3 WAYS

Wrapping up your fish and steaming it in the oven keeps your fish fillets juicy, with the added bonus of all the saucy goodness it produces in the bottom of your paper parcels. Steamed Jasmine Rice (page 178) is the perfect side to make the most of all that delicious sauce.

SWEET CHILLI & LIME PARCELS

SERVES 4, READY IN 20 MINUTES

½ cup sweet chilli sauce
3 tablespoons lime juice
4 × 180 g skinless white fish fillets such as snapper, ling, barramundi or any firm white fish
¼ cup finely sliced spring onions
¼ cup roughly chopped fresh coriander
lime wedges to serve

STEP 1
Preheat the oven to 200°C. Mix the sweet chilli sauce and lime juice in a small bowl.

STEP 2
Cut four 40 cm-long pieces of baking paper. Place a fillet of fish in the centre of each piece of paper and sprinkle over the spring onions and coriander. Bring the long sides of each piece of paper together and twist each of the two short sides to form a Christmas cracker shape (but leave a small opening in the top to pour in your sauce).

STEP 3
Spoon the sweet chilli sauce mixture into your fish parcels and fold over the openings to seal each parcel. Place the parcels on a baking tray and bake for 15 minutes, or until the fish is just cooked through.

STEP 4
Serve the parcels as they are, to be opened at the table, or transfer the fish to individual serving plates, making sure to pour over the sauce. Serve with lime wedges and Steamed Jasmine Rice (page 178).

CORIANDER & GARLIC PARCELS

SERVES 4, READY IN 30 MINUTES

6 coriander roots
2 garlic cloves
½ teaspoon black peppercorns
2 small bunches bok choy,
    quartered
½ red capsicum, finely sliced
4 × 180 g skinless white fish
    fillets such as snapper, ling,
    barramundi or any firm
    white fish
½ cup light soy sauce

STEP 1

Preheat the oven to 200°C. Use a mortar and pestle to pound the coriander roots, garlic and peppercorns to a rough paste.

STEP 2

Cut four 40 cm-long pieces of baking paper. Place even piles of bok choy and capsicum in the centre of each piece of paper. Top with a fish fillet and smear the fish with the coriander and garlic paste. Spoon 2 tablespoons of the soy sauce over each fillet. Bring the long sides of each piece of paper together and twist each of the two short sides to form a Christmas cracker shape, completely enclosing the fish.

STEP 3

Place the parcels on a baking tray and bake for 15 minutes, or until the fish is just cooked through.

STEP 4

Serve the parcels as they are, to be opened at the table, or transfer the fish to individual serving plates, making sure to pour over the sauce. Serve with Steamed Jasmine Rice (page 178).

SOY & GINGER PARCELS

SERVES 4, READY IN 20 MINUTES

1 tablespoon finely grated
    fresh ginger
¼ cup Japanese soy sauce
3 teaspoons sesame oil
4 × 180 g skinless white fish
    fillets, such as snapper, ling,
    barramundi or any firm
    white fish
2 spring onions, finely sliced

STEP 1

Preheat the oven to 200°C. Mix the ginger, soy sauce and sesame oil together and set aside.

STEP 2

Cut four 40 cm-long pieces of baking paper. Place a fillet of fish in the centre of each piece of paper and sprinkle with spring onions. Bring the long sides of each piece of paper together and twist each of the two short sides to form a Christmas cracker shape (but leave a small opening in the top to pour in your sauce).

STEP 3

Spoon the soy sauce mixture into your fish parcels and fold over the openings to seal each parcel. Place the parcels on a baking tray and bake for 15 minutes, or until the fish is just cooked through.

STEP 4

Serve the parcels as they are, to be opened at the table, or transfer the fish to individual serving plates, making sure to pour over the sauce. Serve with Steamed Jasmine Rice (page 178).

CRAB OMELETTE

½ cup cooked crab meat*
¼ cup sliced spring onions
2 tablespoons oyster sauce
4 eggs
1 teaspoon fish sauce
freshly ground black pepper
1 tablespoon vegetable oil
¼ cup bean shoots
1 long red chilli, thinly sliced
2 tablespoons roughly chopped
   fresh coriander

I've noted down 'Serves 2' for this dish because technically it should and will. But this omelette is so, so good – and I mean ridiculously good – it's simply too good to share. Best to keep extra ingredients on hand, just in case.

STEP 1

Gently toss the crab meat and spring onions in a small bowl to combine.

STEP 2

In another small bowl, mix the oyster sauce with 1 teaspoon of water to loosen. Set aside for later.

STEP 3

Whisk together the eggs, fish sauce, 2 tablespoons of water and a generous grinding of pepper in a large bowl.

STEP 4

Heat the vegetable oil in a 25 cm non-stick frying pan over medium–high heat. Add the egg mixture and use a spatula to draw the egg in towards the centre. Swirl the mixture in the pan to allow the uncooked egg to run out towards the edge. Keep doing this until the omelette is almost set.

STEP 5

Sprinkle the crab meat mixture over one half of the omelette. Flip the empty side of the omelette over the crab. Turn out onto a serving plate. Drizzle with spoonfuls of the oyster sauce mixture, then top with bean shoots, chilli and coriander. Share between two – if you can!

* Pre-picked fresh crab meat is available
  at fishmongers and some gourmet delis.

GRILLED LOBSTER WITH KAFFIR LIME BUTTER

SERVES 8, READY IN 20 MINUTES

vegetable oil for greasing
8 × 150 g lobster tails,
  halved lengthways
lime wedges to serve

Kaffir lime butter
250 g butter, softened
10 kaffir lime leaves, stems
  removed, finely sliced
4 garlic cloves, roughly chopped
1 long red chilli, roughly chopped
1 tablespoon fish sauce

I love the fanfare of serving lobster tails for special celebrations. A platter of buttery crustaceans is the perfect way to say 'Merry Christmas', 'Happy Birthday' or 'I love you'.

But please don't relegate my kaffir lime butter to special occasions only. This stuff is wickedly good on prawns, scallops or fish. Make a double batch and keep it in the freezer for flavour emergencies.

STEP 1
Preheat the oven grill to medium–high. Line a baking tray with foil and lightly brush the foil with a little vegetable oil.

STEP 2
To make the kaffir lime butter, place the ingredients in the bowl of a food processor and whizz until smooth. Scoop the butter out into a bowl and refrigerate if not using straight away. Bring to room temperature before using.

STEP 3
Arrange the lobster tails, cut-side down, on the prepared tray. Place under the preheated grill and cook for 3–4 minutes, or until the shells turn orange. Turn the lobster tails over and spread equally with all the butter. Place back under the grill for another 3–4 minutes, or until the lobster is just cooked.

STEP 4
Serve with lime wedges.

THAI RED CURRY–POACHED SALMON

SERVES 4, READY IN 20 MINUTES

1 tablespoon vegetable oil
2 tablespoons red curry paste
2 cups coconut milk
3 tablespoons fish sauce
2 tablespoons shaved palm sugar
4 kaffir lime leaves
100 g (drained weight) canned
   sliced bamboo shoots*
4 × 180 g skinless salmon fillets
fine slices of spring onion
   to serve
Thai basil leaves to serve
1 long red chilli, finely sliced,
   to serve

This recipe is equally impressive as an easy weeknight meal or as a dinner party main course. The secret is to very gently coax your salmon fillets into doing their thing. A barely bubbling sauce will allow your fish to soak up the richly spiced sauce without overcooking. Serve with Steamed Jasmine Rice (page 178), some simply steamed Asian greens or even a creamy pile of mashed potato.

STEP 1

Heat the vegetable oil over medium–high heat in a deep non-stick frying pan large enough to just fit your four salmon fillets. Add the curry paste and cook, stirring, for about a minute, or until fragrant. Add the coconut milk, fish sauce, palm sugar and kaffir lime leaves. Bring to a gentle simmer and cook, stirring, for 2–3 minutes.

STEP 2

Add the bamboo shoots and salmon fillets. Cover with a lid and gently simmer until the salmon is just cooked (about 8 minutes).

STEP 3

Divide the salmon between serving plates and spoon over the curry sauce. Top with spring onion, basil leaves and sliced red chilli.

* Cans of sliced bamboo shoots are available in the Asian section of most major supermarkets or from your Asian grocer.

BURMESE PRAWN CURRY

SERVES 4, READY IN 25 MINUTES

1 tablespoon vegetable oil

500 g tomatoes (about 4 large tomatoes), diced

750 g peeled and deveined raw prawns (about 1.5 kg if you're buying them unpeeled)

2 tablespoons fish sauce

2 tablespoons lime juice

roughly chopped fresh coriander to serve

Curry paste

2 whole dried long red chillies

4 eschallots, roughly chopped

3 garlic cloves, roughly chopped

1 teaspoon turmeric

1 teaspoon vegetable oil

¼ teaspoon sea salt

This very simple curry paste produces a light, delightfully fragrant sauce. Making a double batch of the paste won't take any more time and it means you can freeze it for another night's dinner.

Fresh curry pastes can last up to a month in the freezer but I like to use them up as soon as possible, because they start to lose their complexity and fragrance the longer you leave them.

I like to serve this curry with Steamed Jasmine Rice (page 178) or cooked rice vermicelli noodles.

STEP 1
To make the curry paste, soften the dried chillies in a bowl of hot water for 5 minutes, then roughly chop them. Transfer to the bowl of a small food processor, add the remaining curry paste ingredients and whizz until smooth.

STEP 2
Heat the vegetable oil in a wok over medium–high heat. Add the curry paste and cook, stirring, for about a minute. Add the tomatoes and ½ cup of water. Cover with a lid and simmer for 10 minutes, or until the tomatoes have broken down and the sauce has thickened slightly.

STEP 3
Add the prawns and the fish sauce. Simmer for 2–3 minutes, or until the prawns are cooked. Remove from the heat. Stir through the lime juice and sprinkle over the fresh coriander.

STEP 4
Serve with rice or noodles.

CRUMBED CORIANDER FISH FINGERS

SERVES 4, READY IN 30 MINUTES

2 cups panko breadcrumbs*
1 cup roughly chopped fresh
   coriander
finely grated zest of 1 lemon
2 teaspoons sea salt
1 garlic clove, roughly chopped
½ cup plain flour
3 eggs, lightly whisked
800 g white fish fillets, cut into
   strips about 3 cm wide
vegetable oil for frying
lime wedges to serve

Tartare sauce

½ cup 'Kewpie' (Japanese)
   mayonnaise*
3 tablespoons finely chopped
   cornichons
2 tablespoons finely chopped
   mint leaves

Adding garlic, fresh herbs and lemon zest to the breadcrumb coating in this recipe boosts these fish fingers way above the ordinary. You could also use the same breadcrumb coating to make chicken nuggets or pork schnitzels.

STEP 1

To make the tartare sauce, mix the ingredients in a bowl and set aside until ready to serve.

STEP 2

Place the panko breadcrumbs, coriander, lemon zest, salt and garlic in a food processor and blend until you have fine crumbs. Tip out into a large bowl.

STEP 3

Place the flour and eggs in separate bowls. Dip each strip of fish into the flour, then into the eggs and finally into the breadcrumbs.

STEP 4

Pour the vegetable oil into a large non-stick frying pan to a depth of 1 cm. Place over medium–high heat. Cook the fish fingers for 2–3 minutes on each side, until golden and just cooked. Drain on paper towel.

STEP 5

Serve with lime wedges and tartare sauce.

* Panko is a type of large, flaky breadcrumb that becomes super crispy when fried and is available at most major supermarkets or any Asian grocer.

* 'Kewpie' (Japanese) mayonnaise is available in the Asian section of most major supermarkets.

THAI YELLOW CURRY CRAB

SERVES 4, READY IN 25 MINUTES

3 x 400 g raw blue swimmer crabs

2 tablespoons vegetable oil

1 tablespoon curry powder (look for a mild curry powder with turmeric)

4 garlic cloves, finely chopped

1 brown onion, halved and cut into thin wedges

2 celery stalks, stems sliced and leaves roughly chopped

2 tablespoons fish sauce

2 eggs, lightly whisked

3 spring onions, trimmed and cut into 3 cm batons

This is one of my mum's Thai specialties and a firm family favourite. It's more of a fragrantly spiced, light stir-fry dish than a thick, rich curry, which means the crab itself is the star of the show. Dad and I get that wild look in our eyes as a steaming plate of this hits the table. You've got to be quick at my family table. Your capacity to indulge is inextricably linked to your ability to pull apart crab pieces at the speed of light.

Steamed Jasmine Rice (page 178) or Chinese Sausage & Egg Fried Rice (page 181) would be good sides for your crab.

STEP 1

To prepare the crab, lift the triangular flap under the body and pull off the top part of the shell. Rinse the top shell clean and place in a large bowl. Remove and discard the spongy gills on either side of the body. Use a large knife to cut the body in half and then in half again. Use the back of the knife to lightly crack the legs and claws. Place the crab pieces in the bowl with the top shell. Do the same with the remaining two crabs.

STEP 2

Heat the vegetable oil in a large wok over high heat. Add the curry powder, garlic, onion and sliced celery stems and stir-fry for 2 minutes. Add 1 cup of water and the fish sauce, then toss through the crab pieces. Cover with a lid and simmer for about 10 minutes (give the crab pieces a toss after about 5 minutes), until the crab shells change colour and the meat turns white. Remove the lid and pour the eggs over the crab mixture. Let the egg set for 30 seconds, then toss through the sauce. Remove from the heat and toss through the chopped celery leaves and spring onions. Serve immediately.

KOREAN SEAFOOD PANCAKES

MAKES ABOUT 12, READY IN 30 MINUTES

1½ cups plain flour

1 teaspoon sea salt

3 eggs, lightly whisked

6 spring onions, trimmed, sliced in half lengthways and cut into 6 cm-long strips

vegetable oil for shallow-frying

300 g peeled and deveined raw prawns (about 600 g if you're buying them unpeeled)

1 tablespoon black sesame seeds

3 tablespoons finely sliced spring onions to serve (optional)

Spicy dipping sauce

¼ cup light soy sauce

1 tablespoon rice vinegar

2 teaspoons sesame oil

2 teaspoons white sugar

1 teaspoon gochujang (Korean chilli paste)* or sriracha chilli sauce*

2 tablespoons finely sliced spring onions

Who says you can't have pancakes for dinner? Serve with steamed rice (see Steamed Jasmine Rice on page 178), Wok-fried Asian Greens (see recipe on page 174) or some spicy kimchi (a type of pickled vegetable available from Asian grocers) for a complete meal.

STEP 1

Preheat the oven to 120°C. Line a baking tray with foil and place in the oven to warm.

STEP 2

To make the spicy dipping sauce, whisk the ingredients together until the sugar has dissolved. Pour into a serving bowl and set aside for later.

STEP 3

To make the pancake batter, whisk the flour, salt, eggs and 1 ¼ cups of water in a large bowl until smooth. Gently fold through the strips of spring onion.

STEP 4

Heat enough vegetable oil to just cover the base of a large non-stick frying pan and place over medium–high heat. Pour a ¼ cup of batter into the pan (ensuring there are plenty of spring onions strips in each pancake). Fit as many pancakes as you can (two or three) in the pan. While the batter is still uncooked on the top, gently push 1 heaped teaspoon of chopped prawn pieces into the batter and sprinkle with a pinch of sesame seeds. Cook for 1–2 minutes, or until the underside is golden, then flip each pancake over and cook for another minute. Remove the pancakes and drain on paper towel. Place the cooked pancakes on the prepared baking tray and keep warm in the oven. Repeat this process until you have used all the batter.

STEP 5

Place the pancakes on a serving platter and sprinkle with spring onions (if using). Serve warm with the dipping sauce.

* Gochujang (Korean chilli paste) is a spicy, smoky chilli paste found at most Asian grocers.

* Sriracha chilli sauce is a spicy, tangy chilli condiment. Find it in the Asian or sauce aisle of most supermarkets.

VIETNAMESE PRAWN SALAD

¼ cup raw peanuts

150 g dried rice vermicelli
noodles

800 g whole cooked prawns,
peeled and deveined

1 cup mint leaves, roughly torn

½ cup roughly chopped fresh
coriander

½ cup bean shoots

3 tablespoons fried shallots*

Dressing

4 tablespoons white sugar

4 tablespoons fish sauce

2 tablespoons white vinegar

2 garlic cloves, finely chopped

1 long red chilli, deseeded and
finely chopped

2 tablespoons lime juice

A few extra ingredients you might want to add to make the most of this fragrant, herby salad – a warm summer's night, a chilled glass of white wine and some lovely people to share the meal with.

STEP 1

To make the dressing, place the sugar, fish sauce, vinegar and ¼ cup of water in a small saucepan over high heat. Simmer until the sugar dissolves (about 2 minutes). Stir through the garlic, chilli and lime juice. Set aside until ready to serve.

STEP 2

Place the peanuts in a dry frying pan and toss over high heat until dark golden. Remove from the heat and roughly chop.

STEP 3

Cook the vermicelli noodles in boiling water for 2 minutes, or until tender. Drain and rinse under running water to cool. Use scissors to roughly cut the noodles into shorter lengths. Place the noodles in a large mixing bowl.

STEP 4

Add the prawns, mint, coriander, bean shoots, roasted peanuts and dressing to the noodles. Toss to thoroughly coat all the ingredients with the dressing. Pile onto a serving platter or individual plates, top with the fried shallots and serve.

* Jars or packets of ready-made fried shallots or onions can be bought from the Asian aisle of most supermarkets or an Asian grocer.

THAI GREEN SEAFOOD CURRY

SERVES 4, READY IN 25 MINUTES

1 tablespoon vegetable oil

3 tablespoons Thai green
   curry paste

1 cup coconut cream

4 kaffir lime leaves

2 tablespoons fish sauce

1 tablespoon shaved palm sugar

100 g (drained weight) canned
   sliced bamboo shoots*

200 g peeled and deveined raw
   prawns (about 400 g if you're
   buying them unpeeled)

12 mussels, cleaned and
   beards removed

1 small squid tube (about
   200 g), cleaned and sliced into
   thin rings

1 cup Thai basil leaves (use
   regular basil if you need to)

Just the smell of a Thai green curry simmering away on my stove top feels like a big hug from my mum. The recipes I love the most are those that have made their way to my kitchen through my Thai family heritage and my mum's green curry is one of my most treasured.

STEP 1

Heat the vegetable oil in a saucepan over medium heat. Add the curry paste and cook, stirring, for about a minute, or until fragrant. Add the coconut cream and 1 cup of water and bring to a simmer. Add the kaffir lime leaves, fish sauce and palm sugar. Then add the bamboo shoots, prawns, mussels and squid. Simmer gently for about 5 minutes, or until the prawns and squid have turned opaque and the mussels have opened. Remove from the heat and stir through the basil leaves just before serving.

STEP 2

Serve with Steamed Jasmine Rice (page 178) to mop up all that lovely curry sauce.

* Cans of sliced bamboo shoots are
available in the Asian section of most
major supermarkets or from your
Asian grocer.

PRAWN MEE GORENG

400 g thin pre-cooked
  egg noodles*
2 tablespoons vegetable oil
3 garlic cloves, finely chopped
1 brown onion, halved and
  finely sliced
300 g peeled and deveined raw
  prawns (about 600 g if you're
  buying them unpeeled)
1 cup finely shredded cabbage
2 spring onions, finely sliced
3 tablespoons fried shallots*

Sauce

2 teaspoons sambal oelek*
  (use less if you'd like it mild)
1 teaspoon shrimp paste*
2 tablespoons dark soy sauce
1 tablespoon light soy sauce
1 tablespoon tomato sauce

I like to describe shrimp paste as the Asian version of Vegemite or Marmite. It's smelly and completely foreign if you haven't grown up eating it but, once you've got it into your dish (or on toast, in the case of Vegemite or Marmite), it's a totally different story. The salty, slightly fishy flavour of shrimp paste adds a deep savoury umami richness to stir-fries and curries. You won't even know it's there; just don't smell it before you add it!

STEP 1

Prepare the noodles according to the packet instructions. I find soaking them in boiling water for about 3 minutes, then rinsing them under cold water usually does the trick. Set aside for later.

STEP 2

To make the sauce, whisk all the ingredients together in a small bowl.

STEP 3

Heat the vegetable oil in a wok over high heat. Stir-fry the garlic and onion for about a minute. Add the prawns and stir-fry until just cooked (about 2 minutes). Now add the cabbage, noodles and sauce. Toss and stir-fry for another 2 minutes, until the ingredients are well combined.

STEP 4

Remove from the heat and toss through the spring onions. Pile onto a serving plate and scatter over the fried shallots.

* Packets of pre-cooked egg noodles are available from the Asian section of most supermarkets.

* Jars or packets of ready-made fried shallots or onions can be bought from the Asian aisle of most supermarkets or an Asian grocer.

* Sambal oelek is a spicy paste made from fresh red chillies and can be found in the Asian aisle of some supermarkets or at any Asian grocer.

* Shrimp paste can be found in some major supermarkets or at any Asian grocer.

SOUTH INDIAN FISH CURRY

SERVES 6, READY IN 30 MINUTES

2 tablespoons vegetable oil

1 brown onion, halved and finely sliced

3 garlic cloves

1 tablespoon finely grated fresh ginger

1 long green chilli, finely chopped

6 curry leaves (leave these out if you can't get hold of them)

1 tablespoon ground coriander

2 teaspoons ground cardamom

1 teaspoon black mustard seeds

½ teaspoon chilli powder (or to taste)

¼ teaspoon turmeric

1 teaspoon sea salt

1 tablespoon tomato paste

3 tomatoes, finely chopped

2 cups coconut milk

800 g skinless white fish fillets, cut into thick strips

roughly chopped fresh coriander to serve (optional)

lime wedges to serve (optional)

Indian curries are all about timing. Take the time to soften the onions until they're sticky and sweet. Give your spices a minute or so to toast up in the pan after you add them and keep those tomatoes simmering until they break down and ooze into the curry sauce.

This is a light, creamy and delicately spiced fish curry that would work just as well with prawns.

STEP 1

Heat the vegetable oil in a large saucepan over medium–high heat. Add the onion and cook for at least 5 minutes, until soft. Add the garlic, ginger, chilli and curry leaves and cook for about a minute. Add the coriander, cardamom, mustard seeds, chilli powder, turmeric and salt and cook, stirring, for another minute. Stir through the tomato paste, then add the tomatoes and ¼ cup of water. Simmer on low for 5 minutes, until the tomatoes have softened and dissolved into the curry sauce.

STEP 2

Now add your coconut milk and the fish pieces. Cover and simmer until the fish is just cooked (about 5 minutes).

STEP 3

Remove from the heat and transfer to a serving bowl. Sprinkle with coriander and serve with lime wedges (if using).

SLIGHTLY CHARRY CHAR SIU SALMON

SERVES 4, READY IN 20 MINUTES

4 tablespoons char siu sauce*
1 tablespoon honey
1 tablespoon light soy sauce
2 tablespoons lime juice
4 × 200 g skinless salmon fillets
lime wedges to serve
roughly chopped fresh coriander
   to serve

The sweet char siu sauce and honey in this marinade will start to bubble and catch on the edges of the salmon fillets as they cook, creating a lovely, slightly charred look and flavour. Keep an eye on your salmon and turn down the heat if it starts to brown too quickly. A simple side of Steamed Jasmine Rice or Wok-fried Asian Greens (see recipes on pages 178 and 174 respectively) are friendly accompaniments.

STEP 1

Preheat the oven grill to medium–high. Line a baking tray with foil.

STEP 2

In a large bowl, whisk together the char siu sauce, honey, soy sauce and lime juice.

STEP 3

Dunk each salmon piece in the char siu mixture until well coated and arrange on the lined baking tray. Reserve the remaining marinade.

STEP 4

Place under the preheated grill and cook for 6 minutes. Carefully pull out your baking tray and baste the salmon with the reserved marinade. Return the salmon to the oven and cook for another 6 minutes, until the edges of the salmon are just starting to char and the fish is cooked through. Keep an eye on the heat of your grill and, if the salmon starts to brown too quickly, turn the heat down.

STEP 5

Serve with lime wedges and a sprinkling of fresh coriander.

* Char siu sauce is a sweet and salty Chinese barbecue sauce with a red colour. It comes in jars and is available from the Asian aisle of most supermarkets.

CHICKEN & DUCK

01.	VIETNAMESE CHICKEN SALAD	058
02.	BARBECUED CHICKEN BANH MI	060
03.	BASIC POACHED CHICKEN	062
04.	HAINANESE CHICKEN RICE	064
05.	MISO CHICKEN NOODLE SOUP	066
06.	PANANG CHICKEN CURRY	069

CHICKEN WINGS 3 WAYS

07.	TANDOORI CHICKEN WINGS	071
08.	RENDANG CHICKEN WINGS	072
09.	HOT 'N' SPICY CHICKEN WINGS	072

10.	MUM'S SWEET & SOUR CHICKEN	075
11.	GARAM MASALA CHICKEN	076
12.	KOREAN GRILLED CHICKEN	078
13.	VIETNAMESE LEMONGRASS CHICKEN	080
14.	HOT & SOUR CHICKEN SOUP	081
15.	CHICKEN & EGG DONBURI	082
16.	CHICKEN KARAAGE	084
17.	THAI CHICKEN & GINGER STIR-FRY	087
18.	DUCK NOODLE SALAD	088
19.	DUCK WITH HOISIN PLUM SAUCE	090
20.	DUCK RED CURRY NOODLE SOUP	093

VIETNAMESE CHICKEN SALAD

SERVES 4, READY IN 20 MINUTES

1 large carrot, cut into fine strips
   using a julienne peeler or
   coarsely grated

2 cups shredded cooked chicken
   (leftover roast chicken, poached
   chicken or a barbecued chook
   are all good options)

3 cups finely shredded cabbage

¼ cup finely sliced spring onions

½ cup torn mint leaves

¼ cup roasted peanuts,
   roughly chopped

1 long red chilli, finely sliced

¼ cup fried shallots*

Dressing

¼ cup honey

2 tablespoons white vinegar

4 teaspoons fish sauce

1 eschallot, finely sliced

I am in love with the fresh, fragrant salads of Vietnam. It's that heady mix of pungent fresh herbs, crunchy bits and tangy dressing that does it for me. Serve this salad as a stand-alone meal or as part of a barbecue spread. A meat-free version without the chicken is equally satisfying.

This salad makes a great packed lunch too. Put the fried shallots in a small container to keep them crisp and keep the dressing in a separate small container. Toss the undressed salad and pack it in a zip-lock bag. When you are ready to serve, pour the dressing into the zip-lock bag and give the bag a shake. Empty the salad out onto a plate and top with the crispy fried shallots. The best lunch in a bag you're likely to get!

STEP 1
To make the dressing, whisk all the ingredients together. Set aside until ready to serve.

STEP 2
Combine the carrot, chicken, cabbage, spring onions, mint, peanuts and chilli in a large bowl.

STEP 3
When ready to serve, add the dressing and toss. Pile onto a serving plate and sprinkle with fried shallots.

* Jars or packets of ready-made fried shallots or onions can be bought from the Asian aisle of most supermarkets or an Asian grocer.

BARBECUED CHICKEN BANH MI

¼ cup white vinegar

¼ cup white sugar

1 carrot, cut into fine strips using a julienne peeler or coarsely grated

4 long crusty bread rolls

softened butter for spreading

80 g pork or chicken liver pâté

¼ cup mayonnaise

sriracha chilli sauce* to taste

1 Lebanese cucumber, deseeded and sliced into long, thin batons

200 g shredded barbecued chicken (leftover roast or poached chicken is also good)

trimmed stems of ¼ bunch coriander

1 long red chilli, finely sliced

I remember my very first first banh mi. The crusty bun was filled with all manner of mysterious sliced meats, pâté and crunchy pickled vegetables. Then came the sleek, sweet mayonnaise, followed by a hit of spicy chilli. My quick version of this king of sandwiches uses the humble barbecued chook but you could use any cooked chicken or even leftover roast pork.

STEP 1

Heat the vinegar and sugar in a small saucepan until just simmering. Remove from the heat and toss in your carrot. Transfer to a bowl and set aside in the fridge until ready to serve.

STEP 2

Split the rolls lengthways without cutting all the way through. Lightly butter the rolls, then spread one half with a generous layer of pâté. Spread the other half with mayonnaise and drizzle the whole lot with sriracha sauce to taste.

STEP 3

Take the carrot mixture from the fridge and use tongs to grab a good bit of the carrot (it doesn't matter if it's still a bit warm) and spread it over the rolls. (You'll have plenty of leftover carrot so keep it in the fridge for another day.) Top with cucumber and shredded chicken. Scatter over the coriander stems and chilli slices. Sandwich everything together and serve.

* Sriracha chilli sauce is a spicy, tangy chilli condiment. Find it in the Asian or sauce aisle of most supermarkets.

BASIC POACHED CHICKEN

6 cups chicken stock
5 cm piece ginger, sliced
2 spring onions, cut into
   5 cm batons
2 tablespoons light soy sauce
¼ cup shaoxing (Chinese cooking
   wine)*
4 chicken breasts

There are so many tasty ways to treat a perfectly poached chicken breast – salads, soups, sandwiches, or simply sliced and served with rice and chilli sauce. Allowing the chicken to finish poaching in the residual heat from the hot broth will help to keep the fillets tender and juicy. And, whatever you do, don't forget about that golden poaching liquid. Store it in the freezer and you've got a ready-made broth for noodle soup at your fingertips.

STEP 1
Place the stock, ginger, spring onions, soy sauce and shaoxing in a saucepan over high heat. Bring to the boil then add the chicken breasts. (They should be covered completely with the liquid; if not, add a little water.) Bring back to a gentle simmer. Reduce the heat to medium, cover with a lid and gently simmer for 5 minutes.

STEP 2
Without lifting the lid, remove the pan from the heat and let the chicken rest in the poaching liquid for 12 minutes. Slice the chicken and serve warm, or use for any recipe that requires cooked chicken.

* Shaoxing is a Chinese wine made from fermented rice. Find it at your Asian grocer and some major supermarkets.

THINGS TO DO WITH YOUR BASIC POACHED CHICKEN

✳ Use in sandwiches, salads or soups.
✳ Strain the poaching liquid and freeze it. Use as a flavoursome chicken stock or soup broth.

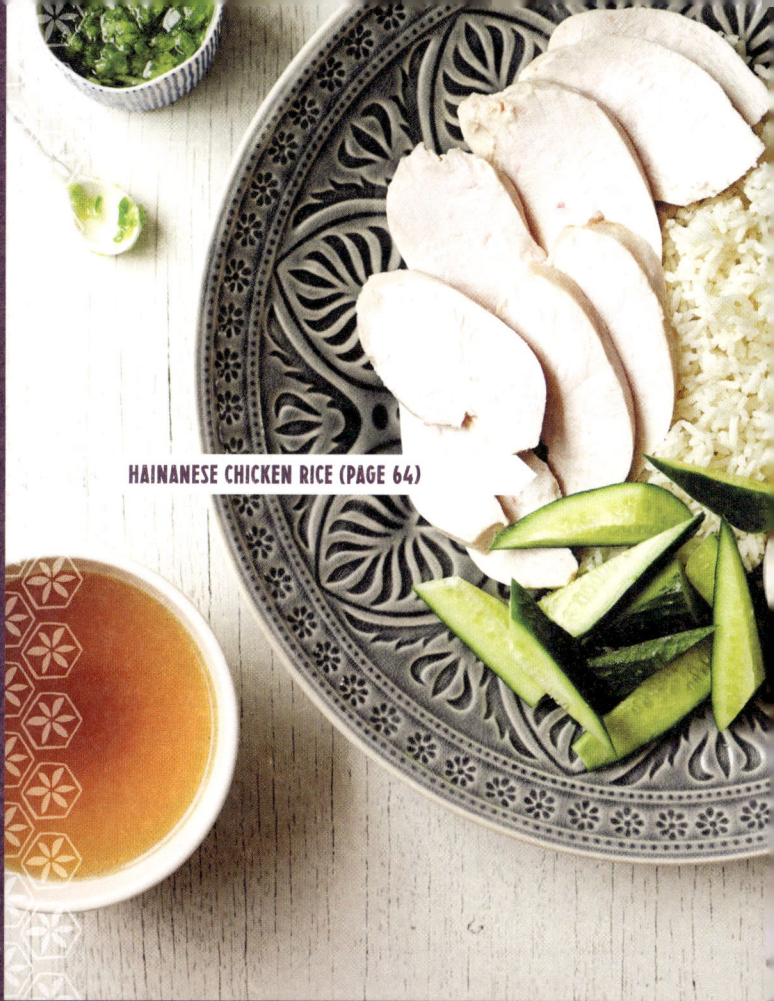

HAINANESE CHICKEN RICE (PAGE 64)

VIETNAMESE CHICKEN SALAD (PAGE 58)

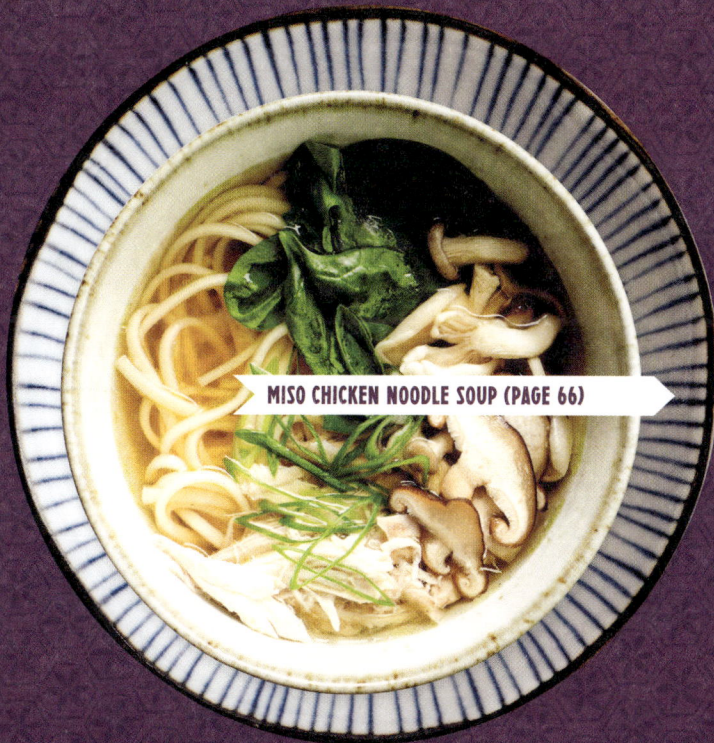

MISO CHICKEN NOODLE SOUP (PAGE 66)

HAINANESE CHICKEN RICE

SERVES 4, READY IN 30 MINUTES

Poached chicken

6 cups chicken stock

5 cm piece ginger, sliced

2 spring onions, cut into
  5 cm batons

2 tablespoons light soy sauce

¼ cup shaoxing (Chinese
  cooking wine)*

4 chicken breasts

sambal oelek* to serve

cucumber wedges to serve

Chicken rice

2 cups long grain rice

3 cups chicken stock

Spring onion and ginger sauce

1 tablespoon finely chopped
  fresh ginger

¾ cup finely sliced spring onions

1 teaspoon sea salt

¼ cup vegetable oil

½ teaspoon sesame oil

The authentic version of this dish takes some time to prepare, with rendered chicken fat flavouring the rice and a whole chicken that needs to be marinated and slowly poached. My version cuts back on the time but still has the delicate, savoury flavours of ginger, spring onion and that all-important, soothing chicken broth.

STEP 1

To poach the chicken, place the stock, ginger, spring onions, soy sauce and shaoxing in a saucepan over high heat. Bring to the boil then add the chicken breasts. (They should be covered completely with the liquid; if not, add a little water.) Bring back to a gentle simmer. Reduce the heat to medium, cover the pan with a lid and gently simmer for 5 minutes.

STEP 2

Without lifting the lid, remove the pan from the heat and let the chicken rest in the poaching liquid for 12 minutes.

STEP 3

While your chicken is poaching, make the chicken rice. Place the rice and stock in a saucepan over medium–high heat and bring to the boil. Reduce the heat to low, cover with a lid and simmer for 12 minutes. Remove from the heat and rest, covered, for 5 minutes. Just before serving, gently fluff up the rice with a fork. You could also use a rice cooker for this.

STEP 4

For the spring onion and ginger sauce, use a mortar and pestle to pound the ginger, spring onions and sea salt to a rough paste. Heat the vegetable and sesame oils in a small saucepan over high heat and, when hot, pour over the spring onion mixture. Stir to combine. Transfer to a small bowl.

STEP 5

Once the chicken is cooked, remove the breasts from the stock. Put the stock back on the heat and bring to the boil.

STEP 6

Slice each chicken breast and serve on a plate with the chicken rice, spring onion and ginger sauce, sambal oelek and cucumber wedges. Ladle the hot poaching liquid into small bowls to slurp up alongside your chicken rice.

* Sambal oelek is a spicy paste made from fresh red chillies and can be found in the Asian aisle of some supermarkets or at any Asian grocer.

* Shaoxing is a Chinese wine made from fermented rice. Find it at your Asian grocer and some major supermarkets.

MISO CHICKEN NOODLE SOUP

250 g dried udon noodles

6 cups chicken stock

1 tablespoon Japanese
  soy sauce

2 tablespoons shiro miso paste*

3 cups cooked and shredded
  chicken (leftover roast chicken
  or poached chicken)

200 g mixed Asian mushrooms
  such as shiitake, oyster and
  shimeji, cut into bite-sized
  chunks

1 small handful (about 50 g) baby
  spinach leaves

¼ cup finely sliced spring onions

When it's cold outside and you've got the sniffles, you need a bowl of this. Seriously soothing!

STEP 1
Cook the udon noodles according to the packet instructions. Drain and divide between the serving bowls.

STEP 2
While your noodles are cooking, place the chicken stock, soy sauce and shiro miso in a saucepan over medium–high heat. Bring to a gentle simmer and cook, stirring occasionally, for about 3 minutes, or until the miso paste dissolves. Add the chicken, mushrooms and baby spinach and cook for a further 2 minutes.

STEP 3
Ladle the soup over the noodles and top with the spring onions.

* Shiro miso is a 'white' or 'sweet' miso, made from mainly rice and soybeans. It is available in the Asian section of most major supermarkets.

PANANG CHICKEN CURRY

SERVES 4, READY IN 15 MINUTES

1 tablespoon vegetable oil

2 tablespoons red curry or
panang curry paste

2 chicken breasts (about 500 g),
very thinly sliced

1 cup coconut cream, plus
3 extra tablespoons to serve

2 tablespoons fish sauce

2 tablespoons shaved palm sugar

6 kaffir lime leaves, stems
removed, finely sliced

1 long red chilli, finely sliced,
to serve (optional)

Panang curries are drier and thicker than their Thai green and red curry cousins. They have the fresh lemongrass, galangal and chilli flavours you get in a Thai red curry but are generally a little sweeter and not as spicy. In Thailand they are often made with thin slices of beef but I find chicken, prawns or tofu are very tasty too. If you happen to come across panang curry paste at an Asian grocer, by all means use it for this recipe, but red curry paste is easier to get hold of and works just as well. Best served with Steamed Jasmine Rice (page 178) to soak up all that lovely curry sauce.

STEP 1

Heat the vegetable oil in a wok or saucepan over medium–high heat and cook the curry paste for about a minute, or until it starts to smell lovely and fragrant.

STEP 2

Add the chicken breasts and stir-fry for about 2–3 minutes, or until the chicken starts to change colour. Add 1 cup of coconut cream, the fish sauce, palm sugar and half the kaffir lime leaves. Simmer for another 6–8 minutes, or until the chicken is cooked.

STEP 3

To serve, spoon the curry into a serving bowl and drizzle over 3 extra tablespoons of coconut cream. Top with the remaining sliced kaffir lime leaves and chilli slices (if using).

CHICKEN WINGS

3 WAYS

The humble chicken wing is the perfect vehicle for soaking up tasty flavourings. A big bowl of steaming wings makes for great party food, or serve them with potato salad or rice for a super tasty, yet easy, weeknight meal

TANDOORI CHICKEN WINGS

SERVES 4, READY IN 20 MINUTES

1 kg chicken wings, cut in half at the joint and tips removed
4 tablespoons tandoori paste
3 tablespoons thick natural yoghurt
2 tablespoons roughly chopped fresh coriander

STEP 1
Preheat the oven to 200°C. Line a baking tray with foil.

STEP 2
Combine the chicken, tandoori paste and yoghurt in a large bowl.

STEP 3
Spread the coated chicken wings out on the lined baking tray and roast in the preheated oven for 25 minutes, or until cooked through.

STEP 4
To serve, sprinkle with fresh coriander.

RENDANG CHICKEN WINGS

SERVES 4, READY IN 30 MINUTES

1 kg chicken wings, cut in half at the joint and tips removed
3 tablespoons rendang curry paste*
1 tablespoon vegetable oil
3 tablespoons finely chopped fresh coriander

Traditionally, rendang is a richly spiced Indonesian meat curry that takes hours to gently simmer and cook. Here, I've used the fragrant paste (usually made with loads of curry spices, ginger, galangal, lemongrass and chillies) as a quick marinade for chicken wings.

STEP 1
Preheat the oven to 200°C. Line a baking tray with foil.

STEP 2
Combine the chicken, curry paste and vegetable oil in a large bowl.

STEP 3
Spread the coated chicken wings out on the lined baking tray and roast in the preheated oven for 25 minutes, or until cooked through.

STEP 4
Sprinkle with coriander and serve.

HOT 'N' SPICY CHICKEN WINGS

SERVES 4, READY IN 20 MINUTES

3 tablespoons tomato sauce
¼ cup sriracha chilli sauce*
2 tablespoons light soy sauce
2 tablespoons brown sugar
1 teaspoon sea salt
1 kg chicken wings, cut in half at the joint and tips removed
1 tablespoon sesame seeds
chilli flakes to taste

STEP 1
Preheat the oven to 200°C. Line a baking tray with foil.

STEP 2
In a large bowl, whisk the tomato sauce, sriracha chilli sauce, soy sauce, brown sugar and salt together. Add the chicken and toss to coat.

STEP 3
Spread the coated chicken wings out on the lined baking tray and roast in the preheated oven for 25 minutes, or until cooked through.

STEP 4
Sprinkle with sesame seeds and chilli flakes to taste.

* Rendang curry paste is available in some major supermarkets or from your Asian grocer.

* Sriracha chilli sauce is a spicy, tangy chilli condiment. Find it in the Asian or sauce aisle of most supermarkets.

MUM'S SWEET & SOUR CHICKEN

4 tablespoons fish sauce

2 tablespoons white vinegar

3 tablespoons white sugar

2 teaspoons cornflour

2 tablespoons vegetable oil

3 garlic cloves, finely chopped

1 brown onion, halved and cut
into thin wedges

500 g chicken thighs, thinly
sliced

1 tomato, cut into small wedges

1 red capsicum, deseeded and
cut into strips

1 small Lebanese cucumber,
sliced on the diagonal

150 g fresh pineapple, cut into
bite-sized pieces

2 spring onions, trimmed and cut
into 2 cm batons

My mum's sweet and sour chicken was the ham and pineapple pizza of my childhood. Mum says I constantly asked for it and could wolf down half the plate just on my own. I still love it. It's much lighter and fresher than the Chinese restaurant version. Chicken was my childhood favourite but this is also super tasty with prawns or tofu.

Cucumber might seem an unusual stir-fry vegetable but I love its ability to hold its crunch yet still soak up bags of sauce. Try it in any of your own stir-fry recipes.

STEP 1
Whisk together the fish sauce, white vinegar and sugar. Set aside for later.

STEP 2
In a separate bowl, combine the cornflour with 3 teaspoons of water to make a paste. Set aside.

STEP 3
Heat the vegetable oil in a wok over high heat. Add the garlic and onion and stir-fry for about a minute. Add the chicken and stir-fry for 3–4 minutes, or until just cooked. Now add the tomato, capsicum, cucumber and pineapple and stir-fry for another 2 minutes. Pour over the fish sauce mixture and toss to combine. Pour over the cornflour mixture and stir-fry for another minute to allow the sauce to thicken.

STEP 4
Remove from the heat and toss through the spring onions to serve.

GARAM MASALA CHICKEN

2 chicken breasts (about 500 g)
2 tablespoons vegetable oil
Indian mango chutney to serve
lime wedges to serve

Marinade

2 tablespoons garam masala
1 tablespoon paprika
¼ teaspoon turmeric
1 teaspoon sea salt
2 garlic cloves, finely grated
  or crushed
¼ cup finely chopped fresh
  coriander
½ cup thick natural yoghurt

My garam masala marinade works wonders on just about anything. Try it with prawns, fish, pork or lamb. My Spiced Indian Rice (page 184), Red Potato Salad (page 168) or a simple green salad would make good sides for this chicken dish.

STEP 1

Cut each chicken breast in half lengthways so you have four thin fillets. Lay the fillets out on a chopping board and cover with baking paper. Use a rolling pin to lightly pound the fillets to an even 1 cm thickness.

STEP 2

To make the marinade, mix all the ingredients in a large bowl. Swish the chicken breasts around in the marinade and let them soak up the flavours for about 5 minutes.

STEP 3

Heat the vegetable oil in a large non-stick frying pan or griddle pan over medium–high heat (don't let the pan get too crazy hot or the spices will burn before your chicken is cooked). Cook the chicken for 3–4 minutes on each side, or until nicely golden and cooked through. Transfer the cooked chicken to a plate and rest for 2 minutes.

STEP 4

Serve the chicken with a dollop of mango chutney and lime wedges to squeeze over for extra tang.

KOREAN GRILLED CHICKEN

1 kg chicken thighs, cut into
quarters

3 tablespoons light soy sauce

1 tablespoon sesame oil

2 tablespoons gochujang (Korean
chilli paste)*

1 tablespoon honey

1 tablespoon finely grated
fresh ginger

3 garlic cloves, finely grated
or crushed

½ cup finely chopped spring
onions

finely grated zest of 1 lemon

1 teaspoon black sesame seeds

¼ teaspoon sea salt

Korean chilli paste or gochujang is a magical ingredient and absolutely worth a trip to an Asian grocer. It's a fermented paste made from chillies, glutinous rice and soy beans. While it sounds fairly ordinary, the flavour of this deep, dark-red paste is far from pedestrian. It's deeply savoury, spicy and just a little sweet.

In Korean cooking it's used as a condiment, marinade, dipping sauce and flavour-booster for braises and soups. It's sold in most Asian grocers and the most common brand comes in a red plastic tub that will keep in your fridge for a few months (that is, if it lasts that long). It's good stuff, but watch out – it's highly addictive!

STEP 1

Preheat the oven grill to medium–high. Line a baking tray with foil.

STEP 2

Place the chicken in a large mixing bowl. Add the soy sauce, sesame oil, gochujang, honey, ginger, garlic and spring onions and mix well.

STEP 3

Spread the chicken out on the lined baking tray. Place under the preheated grill and cook for 15–20 minutes, turning the pieces over after about 7 minutes. You want your chicken pieces to be cooked through with slightly blackened, charry edges. If the chicken starts to burn too quickly, turn the oven grill heat down and move the baking tray lower.

STEP 4

In the meantime, mix the lemon zest, sesame seeds and sea salt together.

STEP 5

Transfer the chicken to a serving plate and sprinkle with the lemon zest mixture. You can serve your chicken with a simple green salad, stir-fried veggies or steamed rice.

* Gochujang (Korean chilli paste) is a spicy, smoky chilli paste that can be found at most Asian grocers.

VIETNAMESE LEMONGRASS CHICKEN

SERVES 4, READY IN 25 MINUTES

600 g chicken thighs,
very thinly sliced

4 tablespoons fish sauce

1 tablespoon white sugar

½ teaspoon cornflour

2 lemongrass stalks (white
part only), bruised and finely
chopped

1 tablespoon vegetable oil

4 garlic cloves, finely chopped

2 long red chillies, deseeded and
finely sliced

1 brown onion, halved and
sliced into thin wedges

1 cup coconut water

¼ cup roughly chopped fresh
coriander to serve

Cooking with coconut water is a genius way of adding a subtle, sweet, coconut flavour. It's a method often used in Vietnamese cooking. Coconut water or coconut juice is the clear liquid from the centre of the coconut, not the milk or cream, which are extracted from the actual coconut flesh. It's best to use fresh coconut juice and I've noticed quite a few major supermarkets now stocking young coconuts in their fresh fruit section. If you can find young coconuts, you're in for a treat – use the juice for this recipe and scoop out the soft coconut flesh for dessert! Most Asian grocers also sell the juice in frozen form.

You'll want plenty of rice (such as Steamed Jasmine Rice on page 178) to soak up all the sweet, sour coconutty sauce.

STEP 1
Combine the chicken, fish sauce, sugar, cornflour and half the lemongrass in a large bowl. Leave to marinate for 10 minutes.

STEP 2
Heat the vegetable oil in a wok over high heat. Add the remaining lemongrass, the garlic, chillies and onion and stir-fry for a minute. Add the chicken mixture and stir-fry for 3–4 minutes, or until the chicken is almost cooked. Add the coconut water and simmer for 5 minutes, or until the chicken is cooked through and the sauce has thickened slightly.

STEP 3
Spoon the chicken and sauce into a large serving bowl. Top with the chopped coriander and serve.

HOT & SOUR CHICKEN SOUP

6 cups chicken stock

1 cup cooked shredded chicken (leftover barbecued or roast chicken is perfect)

1 small carrot, cut into fine strips using a julienne peeler or coarsely grated

200 g shiitake mushrooms, roughly chopped

200 g firm tofu, cut into small cubes

100 g (drained weight) canned sliced bamboo shoots*

½ teaspoon ground black pepper

2 tablespoons dark soy sauce

4 tablespoons light soy sauce

3 tablespoons Chinese black vinegar*

3 tablespoons cornflour

During our family visits to Chinese restaurants, I used to think this was such a magical, mysterious soup. Those steaming little bowls of thick, dark, almost gravy-like broth never failed to mesmerise. Each vinegary, peppery spoonful always made my nose tingle. Chinese black vinegar is the secret ingredient here.

STEP 1

In a large saucepan, place the chicken stock, chicken, carrot, mushrooms, tofu, bamboo shoots, pepper, soy sauces and black vinegar. Bring to the boil over high heat, then reduce the heat to low and simmer for 5 minutes to infuse the flavours.

STEP 2

Place the cornflour in a small bowl and mix with 3 tablespoons of water. Add the flour mixture to the soup and stir. Simmer for another 3–4 minutes to thicken the soup. Serve warm.

* Cans of sliced bamboo shoots are available in the Asian section of most major supermarkets or from your Asian grocer.

* Chinese black vinegar is a dark, complex vinegar that you can find at your Asian grocer.

CHICKEN & EGG DONBURI

SERVES 2, READY IN 30 MINUTES

1 cup Japanese rice
⅓ cup chicken stock
1 teaspoon white sugar
1 tablespoon Japanese soy
  sauce, plus 4 extra teaspoons
  to serve
1 tablespoon vegetable oil
1 brown onion, halved and thinly
  sliced
300 g chicken thighs, thinly
  sliced
3 eggs, lightly whisked
⅓ cup finely sliced spring onions
shichimi togarashi* to serve
  (optional)

Donburi is a Japanese rice bowl dish where the ingredients are usually simmered in a *dashi* broth, a kind of fish stock. Chicken stock makes for an easy substitute in this recipe. I adore the silky, smooth texture of the eggs after they've been cooked in the stock. This is such a comforting weeknight dish. And don't stop at chicken. You can use salmon, prawns, pork or beef – just change the stock accordingly.

STEP 1

Cook the rice according to the packet instructions. Keep it warm and, just before serving, divide between two serving bowls.

STEP 2

While your rice is cooking, combine the chicken stock, sugar and soy sauce in a small bowl.

STEP 3

In a large frying pan, heat the vegetable oil over medium–high heat. Add the onion and stir-fry for 2 minutes. Add the chicken and stir-fry for 4–5 minutes, or until just cooked. Pour the chicken stock mixture into the pan and simmer for about a minute. Drizzle the eggs over the contents of the pan. Cover with a lid and cook for about 3 minutes, or until the egg is just set.

STEP 4

Remove the pan from the heat and divide the chicken and egg mixture between the bowls of rice. Sprinkle with spring onions and shichimi togarashi, if using. Drizzle each bowl with an extra teaspoon or so of soy sauce and serve.

* Shichimi togarashi is a spicy blend of chilli, citrus peel, sesame seeds and nori. You can find it in the Asian section of most major supermarkets or at your Asian grocer.

CHICKEN KARAAGE

SERVES 4 AS A SHARED STARTER, READY IN 30 MINUTES

500 g chicken thighs, cut into
  bite-sized pieces
1 tablespoon finely grated
  fresh ginger
2 garlic cloves, finely grated
  or crushed
1 tablespoon Japanese
  soy sauce
vegetable oil for frying
1 cup plain flour
shichimi togarashi* or chilli flakes
  to serve (optional)
lemon wedges to serve
'Kewpie' (Japanese)
  mayonnaise* to serve

Oh my. What can I say? Fried chicken. Enough said really.

STEP 1
Combine the chicken, ginger, garlic and soy sauce in a large bowl.
Set aside.

STEP 2
Pour enough vegetable oil into a wok or deep frying pan to reach a depth
of 5 cm. Heat to 180°C. If you don't have a cooking thermometer, a cube
of bread will turn golden in 30 seconds when the oil is hot enough.

STEP 3
Place the flour in a large bowl. Take a handful of chicken pieces, dunk
them in the flour and carefully add them to the hot oil. Cook for about
3–4 minutes, or until the chicken is golden and cooked through. Drain
on paper towel. Repeat this process until you have used all the chicken
pieces.

STEP 4
Place the chicken pieces on a serving plate and sprinkle liberally with
shichimi togarashi or chilli flakes, if using. Serve with lemon wedges and
a small bowl of 'Kewpie' (Japanese) mayonnaise for dipping.

* Shichimi togarashi is a spicy blend of
chilli, citrus peel, sesame seeds and nori.
You can find it in the Asian section of
most major supermarkets or at your Asian
grocer.

* 'Kewpie' (Japanese) mayonnaise is
available in the Asian section of most
major supermarkets.

THAI CHICKEN & GINGER STIR-FRY

2 tablespoons vegetable oil

3 garlic cloves, finely chopped

4 cm piece ginger, peeled and cut into matchsticks

2 chicken breasts (about 500 g), thinly sliced

1 red capsicum, deseeded and cut into bite-sized chunks

2 tablespoons oyster sauce

1 tablespoon fish sauce

1 teaspoon white sugar

2 tablespoons finely sliced spring onion to serve

freshly ground black pepper

Ginger is one of those magical ingredients that instantly makes me feel better if I've been feeling poorly. It's believed to be good for your digestive system and helps with throat and nose congestion. But, most importantly, it's ridiculously tasty in any simple stir-fry.

This recipe gives ginger a starring role, so it's essential to get hold of young, plump ginger. Steer clear of those dark, dried up, gnarly-looking ginger pieces and go for one that is smooth-skinned and light-coloured.

STEP 1
Heat the vegetable oil in a wok over high heat. Add the garlic and ginger and stir-fry for a minute. Add the chicken and stir-fry for 3–4 minutes, or until just cooked. Add the capsicum, oyster sauce, fish sauce and sugar. Toss to combine all the ingredients and cook for another minute.

STEP 2
Remove from the heat and toss through the spring onion and generous grindings of pepper just before serving.

DUCK NOODLE SALAD

SERVES 4, READY IN 30 MINUTES

2 duck breasts (about 400 g)
sea salt
100 g rice vermicelli noodles
2 cups finely shredded wombok
1 carrot, cut into fine strips using
    a julienne peeler, or coarsely
    grated
1 eschallot, finely sliced
1 cup mint leaves
1 cup Thai basil leaves (use
    regular basil as a substitute
    if you like)
¼ cup fried shallots*

Dressing
4 tablespoons fish sauce
3 tablespoons sweet chilli sauce
3 tablespoons lime juice
2 teaspoons sesame oil

A sweet and sour dressing always pairs well with rich, fatty slices of duck. But if duck's not your thing, try this salad with chicken, prawns or even fried tofu.

My method for cooking duck breasts aims to do two things: to render out as much fat as possible and to crisp up the skin. Starting the duck, skin-side down, in a dry non-stick pan helps to do both those things. Rendering the fat has nothing to do with any notions of healthfulness but everything to do with having duck fat on hand for cooking potatoes. Hmmm … duck fat potatoes. Strain your duck fat into a sealed container or jar and keep it in the fridge for up to a year, although mine never lasts that long!

STEP 1
Preheat the oven to 180°C. Line a baking tray with foil.

STEP 2
Pat the duck breasts dry with paper towel. Use a sharp knife to score the duck skin at about 0.5 cm intervals. Sprinkle the duck skin liberally with sea salt.

STEP 3
Heat a large non-stick frying pan over high heat. Cook the duck, skin-side down, for 5 minutes. Turn the pieces over and cook for another minute. Then transfer the duck to the lined baking tray and roast in the preheated oven for 5–6 minutes (for medium), or until cooked to your liking. Remove the duck breasts to a plate and set aside to rest for 2 minutes.

STEP 4
While your duck is roasting, cook the noodles in boiling water for 2 minutes, or until tender. Drain and rinse under running water to cool. Use scissors to roughly cut the noodles into shorter lengths.

STEP 5
Place the noodles, wombok, carrot, eschallot, mint and basil in a large bowl.

STEP 6
In a separate bowl, whisk together the dressing ingredients.

STEP 7
When the duck has rested, cut it into thin slices and toss with the noodle mixture and the dressing. Pile onto serving plates and top with crunchy fried shallots.

* Jars or packets of ready-made fried shallots or onions can be bought from the Asian aisle of most supermarkets or an Asian grocer.

DUCK WITH HOISIN PLUM SAUCE

SERVES 4, READY IN 30 MINUTES

4 duck breasts (about 400 g)
sea salt
1 cup chicken stock
¼ cup hoisin sauce
2 tablespoons light soy sauce
1 teaspoon Chinese five-spice
1 tablespoon finely grated
 fresh ginger
4 ripe plums, stones removed
 and quartered (blood plums
 are particularly nice here but
 any plums will do if they're
 not available)
4 whole star anise
2 cinnamon sticks

This little gem of a recipe is so incredibly easy and yet is impressive as a dinner party dish. Serve it as part of a Chinese banquet menu or with steamed rice (such as the Steamed Jasmine Rice on page 178) and Wok-fried Asian Greens (see page 174).

STEP 1
Preheat the oven to 180°C. Line a baking tray with foil.

STEP 2
Pat the duck breasts dry with paper towel. Use a sharp knife to score the duck skin at about 0.5 cm intervals. Sprinkle the duck skin liberally with sea salt.

STEP 3
Heat a large non-stick frying pan over high heat. Cook the duck, skin-side down, for 5 minutes. Turn the pieces over and cook for another minute. Then transfer the duck to the lined baking tray and roast in the preheated oven for 5–6 minutes (for medium), or until cooked to your liking. Remove the duck breasts to a plate and set aside to rest for 2 minutes.

STEP 4
While your duck is roasting in the oven, drain the excess fat from the pan you cooked the duck in. Place over high heat and pour in the chicken stock, using a wooden spoon to scrape up all those yummy duck bits from the base of the pan. Then pour the stock into a small saucepan and place over medium–high heat. Add the hoisin sauce, soy sauce, Chinese five-spice, ginger, plums, star anise and cinnamon sticks. Simmer for 5 minutes, or until the sauce has thickened slightly.

STEP 5
Serve the duck breasts whole or sliced and spoon over loads of the dark plum sauce.

DUCK RED CURRY NOODLE SOUP

SERVES 4, READY IN 30 MINUTES

270 g (1 packet) dried soba
   noodles
2 duck breasts (about 400 g)
sea salt
1 tablespoon vegetable oil
2 tablespoons Thai red
   curry paste
3 cups coconut milk
3 tablespoons fish sauce
4 kaffir lime leaves
2 tablespoons shaved palm sugar
2 tablespoons lime juice
2 bunches bok choy, trimmed
   and thinly sliced
2 eschallots, finely sliced
½ cup roughly chopped
   fresh coriander
¼ cup finely sliced spring onions
½ cup Thai basil leaves (use
   regular basil if you need to)
1 long red chilli, finely sliced,
   to serve

Growing up with a Thai mother meant Asian food was never in short supply in our house. Even now, I'm still enthralled by the delicate balance of flavours that Thai dishes produce. It seems impossible that such big flavours like spicy red chillies, fishy fish sauce, tangy lime and creamy coconut can work together so beautifully, but they do. It's quite simply magical.

STEP 1
Preheat the oven to 180°C. Line a baking tray with foil.

STEP 2
Cook the soba noodles according to the packet instructions. Drain and divide between four serving bowls.

STEP 3
Pat the duck breasts dry with paper towel. Use a sharp knife to score the duck skin at about 0.5 cm intervals. Sprinkle the duck skin liberally with sea salt.

STEP 4
Heat a large non-stick fying pan over high heat. Cook the duck, skin-side down, for 5 minutes. Turn the pieces over and cook for another minute. Then transfer the duck to the lined baking tray and roast in the oven for 5–6 minutes (for medium), or until cooked to your liking. Remove the duck breasts to a plate and set aside to rest for 2 minutes.

STEP 5
While your duck is roasting in the oven, heat the vegetable oil in a large saucepan over medium heat. Add the curry paste and cook, stirring, for about a minute, or until fragrant. Add the coconut milk, fish sauce, kaffir lime leaves, palm sugar and 1 cup of water. Bring to a gentle simmer and cook, stirring, for 2–3 minutes. Stir through the lime juice.

STEP 6
Thinly slice the rested duck breasts. Divide the duck, bok choy and eschallots evenly between the bowls of noodles. To serve, pour over the red curry soup and top with coriander, spring onions, basil and chilli.

PORK 豚

01.	CHAR SIU PORK	096
02.	TONKATSU	098
03.	PORK & PRAWN HOKKIEN MEE	100
04.	DAN DAN NOODLES	102
05.	THAI PORK NOODLES IN GRAVY	103
06.	THAI GRILLED PORK SALAD	105
07.	ASIAN PORK BURGERS	106
08.	VIETNAMESE PORK & EGG RICE	109
09.	SRIRACHA EGG & HAM CUPS	110
10.	STICKY PORK NOODLE SALAD	112
11.	PORK & EGGPLANT STIR-FRY	115
12.	SICHUAN PORK & GREEN BEANS	116
13.	CHAR SIU PORK NOODLE SOUP	118
14.	SPICY KOREAN PORK	120

CHAR SIU PORK

½ cup hoisin sauce

¼ cup tomato sauce

2 tablespoons shaoxing (Chinese cooking wine)*

2 tablespoons light soy sauce

1 tablespoon honey

¼ teaspoon Chinese five-spice

800 g pork belly, skin removed, cut into 4 cm-wide strips

Char siu pork is that red-roasted pork you may have seen hanging in the windows of Cantonese restaurants. The traditional version is marinated overnight and you could certainly do this if you've got the time. If not, just dunk and roast.

Your choice of pork belly is important here. Select a nice thick slab with decent layers of meat and only thin layers of fat. I find Asian butchers tend to have the best pork belly.

Use your char siu pork in stir-fried noodle dishes, fried rice and soups, or simply serve it with rice and cucumber.

STEP 1

Place a baking tray lined with foil in your oven and preheat at 220°C.

STEP 2

Combine the hoisin sauce, tomato sauce, shaoxing, soy sauce, honey and five-spice in a large bowl. Add the pork belly strips and squish around until well coated.

STEP 3

Carefully slide out your hot baking tray. Lift the pork belly strips out of the marinade and arrange them on the tray, leaving a gap between each piece. Reserve the leftover marinade.

STEP 4

Roast the pork in the oven for 10 minutes, then baste generously with 2 tablespoons of the marinade (reserve remaining marinade). Roast for a further 10 minutes, until the edges of the pork are slightly charred.

STEP 5

While your pork is roasting for the last 10 minutes, pour the remaining marinade into a small saucepan and stir through 2 tablespoons of water. Place the saucepan over medium–high heat and simmer for about 2 minutes to thicken slightly. Set aside until the pork is cooked.

STEP 6

Remove the pork from the oven and brush liberally with the cooked marinade mixture. Now your pork is ready to be sliced and served as you wish.

Shaoxing is a Chinese wine made from fermented rice. Find it at your Asian grocer and some major supermarkets.

TONKATSU

SERVES 4, READY IN 25 MINUTES

½ cup plain flour
2 eggs, lightly whisked
2 cups panko breadcrumbs*
4 × 125 g pork loin cutlets, rind
  and fat trimmed
vegetable oil for shallow-frying
tonkatsu sauce* to serve

I think of tonkatsu as a Japanese-style schnitzel. You've got the crispy crumbed coating and that juicy pork within. Japanese tonkatsu sauce is a non-negotiable part of this dish for me but any good barbecue sauce will do at a pinch. My Red Potato Salad on page 168 works well as a side here but a bowl of steamed rice or a green salad is good too.

STEP 1

To crumb the cutlets, place the flour, egg and breadcrumbs into three separate bowls. Dip each pork cutlet into the flour, then into the egg and finally coat with breadcrumbs.

STEP 2

Heat enough vegetable oil to cover the base of a large non-stick frying pan and place over medium–high heat. Cook the crumbed cutlets for 4 minutes on each side, or until golden and just cooked through. Drain on paper towel.

STEP 3

Serve the cutlets with a drizzle of tonkatsu sauce and your choice of sides.

* Panko is a type of large, flaky breadcrumb that becomes super crispy when fried and is available at most major supermarkets or any Asian grocer.

* Tonkatsu sauce is a Japanese-style barbecue sauce usually served with this crumbed pork and available in some major supermarkets or at Asian grocers.

PORK & PRAWN HOKKIEN MEE

SERVES 4, READY IN 25 MINUTES

400 g thin pre-cooked
   egg noodles*

3 tablespoons dark soy sauce

3 tablespoons light soy sauce

½ cup chicken stock

3 teaspoons white sugar

2 teaspoons cornflour

1 tablespoon vegetable oil

100 g bacon, diced

1 teaspoon shrimp paste

150 g peeled and deveined raw
   prawns (about 300 g if you're
   buying them unpeeled)

1 cup finely shredded cabbage

1 bunch bok choy, trimmed
   and finely sliced

Garlic-marinated pork

200 g pork belly, skin removed,
   cut into 3 cm-wide strips,
   then thinly sliced

4 garlic cloves, finely grated
   or crushed

1 tablespoon light soy sauce

1 tablespoon oyster sauce

1 teaspoon sesame oil

1 teaspoon cornflour

A big bowl of steaming noodles is one of my favourite comfort foods. The traditional version of this dish uses fried cubes of pork fat as a garnish (naughty I know, but incredibly tasty). I've used bacon here instead to add some porky goodness and a slight smokiness.

STEP 1

Combine the ingredients for the garlic-marinated pork and set aside while you prepare everything else.

STEP 2

Prepare the egg noodles according to the packet instructions. I find soaking them in boiling water for about 3 minutes, then rinsing them under cold water usually does the trick. Set aside for later.

STEP 3

Whisk together the dark and light soy sauces, the chicken stock and sugar. Set aside.

STEP 4

In a separate bowl, combine the cornflour and 3 teaspoons of water. Set aside.

STEP 5

Heat the vegetable oil in a wok over high heat. Add the bacon and cook for 2 minutes until crispy. Add the shrimp paste and stir-fry until just dissolved. Next, add the garlic-marinated pork and the prawns and stir-fry for 3–4 minutes, or until just cooked. Add the cabbage and bok choy and stir-fry for another minute. Now toss through the noodles and soy sauce mixture and stir-fry for another minute. Add the cornflour mixture and stir-fry for another minute, until the sauce has thickened slightly.

STEP 6

Remove from the heat and serve.

* Packets of pre-cooked egg noodles are available from the Asian section of most supermarkets.

DAN DAN NOODLES

SERVES 4, READY IN 30 MINUTES

1 teaspoon Sichuan
  peppercorns*
270 g dried udon noodles
4 garlic cloves, roughly chopped
4 cm piece ginger, peeled and
  roughly chopped
2 tablespoons smooth peanut
  butter
3 tablespoons vegetable oil
2 dried long red chillies (finely
  chopped for super hot or left
  whole for mild)
1 cinnamon stick
2 whole star anise
500 g pork mince
1 tablespoon Chinese
  black vinegar*
¼ cup light soy sauce
1½ cups chicken stock
3 tablespoons sesame oil
1 teaspoon white sugar
roughly chopped fresh coriander
  to serve

This dish is thought to have come from the street vendors of Sichuan province in China. The vendors are said to have rested a long pole (called 'dan dan') across their shoulders to balance the noodles on one end and the sauce at the other.

Traditionally, sesame paste would have been used, but I find peanut butter an easy substitute. You can make this dish as hot or mild as you like. If you like a fiery kick, chop up the dried chillies before adding them. Keep them whole for a mildly spicy dish or, if chilli is not your thing, simply leave them out altogether.

STEP 1

Place the Sichuan peppercorns in a small frying pan over high heat. Cook, shaking the pan every so often, for about 2 minutes, or until fragrant. Transfer the peppercorns to a mortar and use a pestle to grind them to a fine powder.

STEP 2

Cook the udon noodles according to the packet instructions. Drain and rinse under running water to cool. Divide between the serving bowls.

STEP 3

Meanwhile, use a mortar and pestle to pound the garlic and ginger to a smooth paste. Stir through the peanut butter.

STEP 4

Heat the vegetable oil in a large frying pan over medium–high heat and cook the chilli, cinnamon and star anise for about 2 minutes. Add the pork mince and stir-fry for 3–4 minutes, until the pork is just cooked. Stir through the garlic–peanut paste, ground Sichuan pepper, vinegar, soy sauce, chicken stock, sesame oil and sugar. Simmer for 5 minutes to thicken.

STEP 5

Top the noodles with the soupy pork mixture and sprinkle over the fresh coriander. Serve warm.

* Sichuan peppercorns are available in the spice section of some major supermarkets or at your Asian grocer.

* Chinese black vinegar is a dark, complex vinegar that you can find at your Asian grocer.

THAI PORK NOODLES IN GRAVY

SERVES 4, READY IN 25 MINUTES

1 tablespoon vegetable oil
600 g fresh rice noodles, cut into
  strips about 3 cm wide*
2 teaspoons dark soy sauce
300 g pork fillet, very thinly sliced
1 tablespoon vegetable oil
3 garlic cloves, finely chopped
2 bunches (about 200 g) pak
  choy (or any other Asian green
  vegetable), roughly sliced
1 cup chicken stock
1 tablespoon oyster sauce
1 tablespoon fish sauce
ground white pepper
chilli flakes to serve

Chilli vinegar
¼ cup white vinegar
2 long red chillies, finely sliced

Marinade
2 tablespoons fish sauce
1 tablespoon cornflour
1 teaspoon sugar

'Rad naa moo' or pork noodles in gravy are a kerbside specialty in Bangkok. The fresh rice noodles are stained black by a quick wok toss with dark, syrupy soy sauce. The final dish sees those charry noodles swimming in a thick, soupy, porky sauce. As with a lot of Thai dishes, the secret to authentic flavours comes from not skimping on the condiments. When you order this dish from a street cart, there are always chilli vinegar and chilli flakes to add to your noodles at will.

STEP 1
Combine the ingredients for the chilli vinegar in a small serving bowl and set aside.

STEP 2
Whisk together the marinade ingredients and 1 tablespoon of water in a large bowl. Add the pork slices and mix to combine thoroughly. Set aside for later.

STEP 3
Cook your noodles first. Heat 1 tablespoon of vegetable oil in a wok over high heat. Add the noodles and soy sauce and toss for 1–2 minutes, until the noodles are just staring to char. Transfer the noodles to a large serving plate.

STEP 4
Place the wok back over high heat and add 1 tablespoon of vegetable oil. Add the garlic and stir-fry for 30 seconds. Add the marinated pork and stir-fry for about 2 minutes, until the pork is almost cooked. Toss through the pak choy (or other green vegetable), then add the chicken stock, oyster sauce and fish sauce. Stir-fry for another minute or so, until the sauce is thick and shiny.

STEP 5
Spoon the pork and gravy mixture over the noodles. Sprinkle with white pepper and serve with chilli flakes and chilli vinegar so that everyone can add their own to taste.

Fresh rice noodles are available at Asian grocers. If you're using them straight from the fridge they'll be stiff, so nuke them in the microwave for 30 seconds to soften them before using.

THAI GRILLED PORK SALAD

SERVES 4, READY IN 25 MINUTES

1 tablespoon raw rice

4 x 150 g pork scotch steaks
   (fillet or loin will do at a pinch)

1 tablespoon vegetable oil

½ teaspoon sea salt

freshly ground black pepper

2 eschallots, finely sliced

½ cup finely sliced spring onions

½ cup roughly torn mint leaves

Dressing

3 tablespoons lime juice

4 tablespoons fish sauce

2 teaspoons sugar

2 teaspoons chilli flakes (or to
   taste)

In Thailand this dish is called 'nam tok moo', which translates literally as 'waterfall pork'. The name supposedly refers to the juiciness of the meat, so it's important to choose the right cut of pork. I prefer pork scotch steaks, which come from a cut that's also called 'pork shoulder' or 'boston butt'. This cut has a nice fat marbling, which will keep your pork juicy while it cooks. Fillet or loin of pork will also do, but be careful not to overcook these cuts as they tend to dry out. In Thailand this salad is traditionally served warm with steamed or sticky rice but if you're serving it on its own as a stand-alone salad you may want to double the quantities.

STEP 1

Cook the raw rice in a dry frying pan over high heat, shaking the pan often, for 4 minutes, or until golden brown. Then use a mortar and pestle to grind the toasted rice to a fine powder.

STEP 2

To make the dressing, whisk the ingredients together and set aside until ready to serve.

STEP 3

In a large bowl, toss the pork with the vegetable oil, sea salt and a generous grinding of black pepper.

STEP 4

Heat a barbecue plate or griddle pan over high heat. Cook the pork for 4–5 minutes on each side, until just cooked through. Remove from the heat, rest for 2 minutes, then thinly slice.

STEP 5

In a large bowl, toss the pork slices with the toasted rice powder, eschallots, spring onions, mint and the dressing. Serve warm.

ASIAN PORK BURGERS

vegetable oil for brushing
softened butter for spreading
6 burger buns, cut in half
100 g mixed salad leaves
2 tomatoes, thinly sliced

Pork patties
500 g pork mince
1 egg
2 garlic cloves, finely chopped
finely grated zest of 1 lime
½ cup finely sliced spring onions
¼ cup roughly chopped fresh
   coriander
½ cup panko breadcrumbs*
2 teaspoons sea salt

Chilli mayo
½ cup 'Kewpie' (Japanese)
   mayonnaise*
2 teaspoons sambal oelek*

Geez, I love a good burger. I often make a double batch of this burger mixture and freeze it in ready-made patties. You can also roll the pork mixture into little meatballs and serve it as a party canapé with a sweet chilli dipping sauce.

STEP 1
Preheat the oven grill to medium–high.

STEP 2
Place all the ingredients for your Thai-style pork patties in a food processor and pulse until combined. Form into six 2 cm-thick patties.

STEP 3
Heat a large frying pan or barbecue grill plate to high. Brush the patties with vegetable oil and cook for 3–4 minutes on each side, or until just cooked through.

STEP 4
While your patties are cooking, spread some butter on the cut side of each bun half. Lay the buns on a baking tray, cut-side up, and place under the preheated oven grill for 2 minutes, or until toasty and golden. Alternatively, grill the buns on the barbecue.

STEP 5
To make the chilli mayo, mix the 'Kewpie' (Japanese) mayonnaise with the sambal oelek and set aside.

STEP 6
Now to assemble your burgers. Spread dollops of chilli mayo on the cut sides of the burger buns. Top the bottom half of each bun with salad leaves, slices of tomato, a pork patty and bun tops. Dig in!

* Panko is a type of large, flaky breadcrumb that becomes super crispy when fried and is available at most major supermarkets or any Asian grocer.

* 'Kewpie' (Japanese) mayonnaise is available in the Asian section of most major supermarkets.

* Sambal oelek is a spicy paste made from fresh red chillies and can be found in the Asian aisle of some supermarkets or at any Asian grocer.

VIETNAMESE PORK & EGG RICE

2 cups long grain rice
4 × 150 g pork scotch steaks
freshly ground black pepper
3 tablespoons vegetable oil
4 eggs
2 tomatoes, sliced, to serve
1 Lebanese cucumber, sliced,
  to serve

Marinade
3 tablespoons fish sauce
1 tablespoon white sugar
¼ teaspoon turmeric
2 garlic cloves, finely grated
  or crushed

Dressing
3 tablespoons white sugar
3 tablespoons fish sauce
2 tablespoons white vinegar
2 garlic cloves, finely chopped
1 long red chilli, deseeded and
  finely chopped
2 tablespoons lime juice

For this recipe I like to use pork scotch steaks, which come from a juicy cut that's also called 'pork shoulder' or 'boston butt'. You could also use pork loin steaks here but be careful not to overcook them as they have less fat and can easily dry out.

STEP 1
Start your rice first. Place the rice in a medium saucepan with 3 cups of water over high heat. Bring to the boil, then reduce the heat to low, cover and cook for 12 minutes, giving it a stir after about 6 minutes. Remove from the heat and let the rice stand, covered, for 5 minutes. Just before serving, fluff up the rice with a fork. You could also use a rice cooker for this.

STEP 2
In a large bowl, whisk together the marinade ingredients until well combined.

STEP 3
Lay the pork scotch steaks out on a chopping board and cover with baking paper. Use a rolling pin or meat mallet to lightly pound the steaks until they are 0.5 cm thick. Place the pork in the marinade and toss to coat. Set aside to marinate while you make the dressing.

STEP 4
To make the dressing, heat the sugar, fish sauce and white vinegar over high heat for 2–3 minutes, or until the sugar dissolves. Stir through the garlic, chilli and lime juice. Set aside until ready to serve.

STEP 5
Heat 1 tablespoon of the vegetable oil in a large non-stick frying pan over medium–high heat and cook the pork for 3–4 minutes on each side (in batches if necessary), until just cooked through. Remove from the heat and rest for 2 minutes.

STEP 6
While your pork is resting, make four fried eggs. Heat the remaining 2 tablespoons of vegetable oil in a clean non-stick frying pan and fry the eggs until cooked to your liking.

STEP 7
Divide the rice, pork, fried egg, tomatoes and cucumber among four serving plates. Top the whole lot with generous spoonfuls of the dressing.

SRIRACHA EGG & HAM CUPS

MAKES 6, READY IN 20 MINUTES

1 tablespoon vegetable oil
6 large, thin slices ham
6 eggs
3 teaspoons sriracha chilli
    sauce* (more or less to taste)
¼ cup roughly chopped fresh
    coriander, plus extra to serve
¼ cup finely sliced spring onions
¼ cup grated cheddar

These little cups of goodness make a great breakfast but are also good as a takeaway lunch or a picnic option. If you're dealing with palates sensitive to chilli, you could opt for a mild sweet chilli sauce or Japanese tonkatsu sauce (a type of barbecue sauce)* instead of the sriracha chilli sauce.

STEP 1
Preheat the oven to 180°C.

STEP 2
Brush a 6-hole muffin pan with vegetable oil.

STEP 3
Drape one slice of ham into each muffin hole (you will have some ham overhang here, which is fine). Crack an egg into each ham-lined muffin hole. Top each egg with half a teaspoon of sriracha sauce, then sprinkle with coriander, spring onions and finally the cheese.

STEP 4
Bake in the preheated oven for about 14 minutes, or until the whites are just set but still wobbly. Cook for a minute or two longer if you like your eggs firm. Loosen each bundle with a butter knife and use the ham overhang to help pull them out. Sprinkle with extra chopped coriander and serve warm or cold.

* Tonkatsu sauce is a Japanese-style barbecue sauce, available in some major supermarkets or at Asian grocers.

* Sriracha chilli sauce is a spicy, tangy chilli condiment. Find it in the Asian or sauce aisle of most supermarkets.

STICKY PORK NOODLE SALAD

SERVES 4, READY IN 25 MINUTES

180 g dried rice vermicelli
noodles
1 tablespoon sesame oil
1 carrot, cut into fine strips
using a julienne peeler or
coarsely grated
1 cup roughly chopped
fresh coriander
4 tablespoons honey
¼ cup light soy sauce
2 teaspoons dark soy sauce
2 tablespoons lime juice
2 tablespoons vegetable oil
3 garlic cloves, finely chopped
1 red onion, thinly sliced
500 g pork belly, skin removed,
cut into 4 cm-wide strips,
then thinly sliced
1 Lebanese cucumber,
sliced, to serve
lime wedges to serve

Sticky pork makes me weak at the knees. I find it difficult to get all those glistening little gems of porky goodness from the pan to the table without some going astray. This is the type of salad to serve warm when that heavenly, sticky pork is at its best.

STEP 1

Cook the vermicelli noodles in boiling water for 2 minutes, or until tender. Drain and rinse under running water to cool. Use scissors to roughly cut the noodles into shorter lengths and transfer to a large bowl. Toss the noodles with sesame oil, carrot and coriander. Divide between four serving bowls.

STEP 2

Whisk the honey, light soy sauce, dark soy sauce and lime juice together. Set aside until ready to use.

STEP 3

Heat the vegetable oil in a wok over high heat. Add the garlic and red onion and stir-fry for about a minute. Add the pork and stir-fry for another 2 minutes. Add the honey mixture and let everything bubble away, uncovered, for 5 minutes, or until the pork is cooked and the sauce has thickened slightly.

STEP 4

Spoon the warm pork and sauce over the noodles. Serve with cucumber slices and lime wedges to squeeze over just before eating.

PORK & EGGPLANT STIR-FRY

2 tablespoons vegetable oil

4 garlic cloves, roughly chopped

2 bird's eye chillies, finely sliced
(use more or less to taste)

300 g pork mince

1 large eggplant (about 400 g),
cut into rough 2 cm cubes

2 tablespoons fish sauce

3 tablespoons oyster sauce

1 cup Thai basil leaves (use
regular basil if you need to)

One of the secrets of Thai cooking is the last-minute addition of Thai basil in stir-fries and curries. And we're not talking about a measly little sprinkling of basil that's more garnish than major ingredient. A big cupful of Thai basil is what you want.

If Thai basil is hard to come by, use regular sweet basil instead. You won't get the same aniseed flavour but you will still get that nice, fresh, herby hit.

STEP 1

Heat the vegetable oil in a wok or large frying pan over high heat. Add the garlic and chilli and stir-fry for 1 minute. Add the pork mince and stir-fry for 3 minutes, until almost cooked. Add the eggplant and toss to combine. Add 2 tablespoons of water and cover with a lid for 2 minutes to briefly steam the eggplant. Remove the lid, add the fish sauce and oyster sauce and stir-fry for 3–4 minutes, or until the eggplant is soft. Toss through the basil leaves.

STEP 2

Remove from the heat and serve.

SICHUAN PORK & GREEN BEANS

2 tablespoons dried shrimp*

100 g pork mince

2 tablespoons vegetable oil

6 whole dried long red chillies
 (or to taste)

4 garlic cloves, finely chopped

500 g green beans, trimmed

4 tablespoons light soy sauce

¼ teaspoon white sugar

1 teaspoon sesame oil

Marinade

1 tablespoon light soy sauce

2 tablespoons shaoxing
 (Chinese cooking wine)*

½ teaspoon cornflour

I find this simple pork and bean dish highly addictive. It's the addition of those sweet little nuggets of chopped dried shrimp that make all the difference here. Try using chicken, beef or turkey mince instead of the pork; they're all tasty substitutes.

The dried red chillies are added whole into this dish so that when they hit the hot oil they infuse a medium level of chilli heat. But feel free to use fewer chillies or even leave them out altogether.

STEP 1

Place the dried shrimp in a small bowl and cover with boiling water. Soak for 3 minutes to soften. Drain and finely chop.

STEP 2

Combine the pork mince with the marinade ingredients in a bowl and set aside while you heat up your wok.

STEP 3

Heat the vegetable oil in a wok over high heat. Add the chillies and garlic and stir-fry for 1 minute. Add the softened dried shrimp and marinated pork mince. Stir-fry for 3–4 minutes, or until the pork is just cooked. Add the green beans, soy sauce, sugar and ⅓ cup of water. Toss to coat, then cover with a lid and let everything simmer away for 2–3 minutes. Stir through the sesame oil, then remove from the heat and serve.

* Packets of dried shrimp are available in the Asian section of most major supermarkets or from an Asian grocer.

* Shaoxing is a Chinese wine made from fermented rice. Find it at your Asian grocer and some major supermarkets.

CHAR SIU PORK NOODLE SOUP

400 g thin pre-cooked
  egg noodles*
6 cups chicken stock
7 cm piece ginger, sliced
2 spring onions, trimmed and cut
  into 5 cm batons, plus ¼ cup
  finely sliced spring onions
  to garnish
2 tablespoons light soy sauce
¼ cup shaoxing (Chinese
  cooking wine)*
200 g sliced Chinese char
  siu pork*
4 small bunches bok choy,
  quartered
hoisin sauce to serve
sambal oelek* to serve

Sliced meats from a Cantonese restaurant make whipping up dinner so incredibly easy. I love the sweet, roasted smell of those restaurants with the lacquered, roasted ducks and crispy pork in the windows. You can take your pick from peking duck, char siu pork, steamed white chicken or roasted pork. Any of these options would work well in this noodle soup. You could also make your own quick version of char siu pork using my recipe on page 96.

STEP 1

Prepare the noodles according to the packet instructions. I find soaking them in boiling water for about 3 minutes, then rinsing them under cold water usually does the trick. Divide between four serving bowls.

STEP 2

Place the chicken stock, ginger, spring onion batons, soy sauce and shaoxing in a saucepan over high heat and bring to the boil. Reduce the heat to medium and simmer for 5 minutes. Scoop out the ginger and the spring onions with a slotted spoon.

STEP 3

Top the noodles with pork slices and bok choy. Pour over the hot chicken stock mixture. Garnish with finely sliced spring onions and serve with hoisin sauce and sambal oelek on the side to add to your soup at will.

* Packets of pre-cooked egg noodles are available from the Asian section of most supermarkets.

* Shaoxing is a Chinese wine made from fermented rice. Find it at your Asian grocer and some major supermarkets.

* Chinese char siu pork is the red roasted pork available from Cantonese restaurants. You can also make your own Char Siu Pork (see page 96).

* Sambal oelek is a spicy paste made from fresh red chillies and can be found in the Asian aisle of some supermarkets or at any Asian grocer.

SPICY KOREAN PORK

500 g pork fillet, very thinly sliced
1 tablespoon vegetable oil
1 brown onion, halved and cut
  into thin wedges
finely grated zest of 1 lemon
2 spring onions, trimmed and
  cut into 3 cm batons
1 teaspoon sesame seeds

Marinade
3 tablespoons gochujang
  (Korean chilli paste)*
1 tablespoon light soy sauce
2 teaspoons white sugar
2 garlic cloves, finely chopped
1 teaspoon finely grated
  fresh ginger
1 tablespoon sesame oil

I've gone on about my love for gochujang (Korean chilli paste) earlier in this book (see Korean Grilled Chicken, page 78), but here we go again – it's epic. I love it, and I love this spicy Korean pork dish just as much.

There are a couple of ways I like to serve this dish. Steamed rice and some store-bought kimchi make a good match. Or for a 'make-your-own adventure' type of dinner I'll often prepare a platter of lettuce leaves, sliced cucumber, finely julienned carrot, fresh coriander, mint leaves and bean shoots. Each person can then take a lettuce leaf and fill it with the spicy pork and their choice of vegetables.

STEP 1
In a large bowl, mix together the marinade ingredients.

STEP 2
Add the pork slices to the marinade and toss to coat.

STEP 3
Heat the vegetable oil in a wok over high heat. Add the onion and stir-fry for 1 minute. Add the pork slices and marinade and stir-fry for 3–4 minutes, until the pork is just cooked. Remove from the heat and toss through the lemon zest and spring onions.

STEP 4
Pile the pork onto a serving plate and sprinkle with sesame seeds. Serve with steamed rice or as a filling for lettuce leaf cups.

* Gochujang (Korean chilli paste) is a spicy, smoky chilli paste found at most Asian grocers.

BEEF & LAMB

01.	STEAK WITH MISO BUTTER	124
02.	KOREAN STEAK SANDWICH	126
03.	SOY—GINGER EYE FILLET STEAKS	128
04.	VIETNAMESE BEEF NOODLE SALAD	129
05.	ROAST PEPPER BEEF WITH PONZU	131
06.	BEEF PHO	132
07.	THAI BEEF SALAD	134
08.	VIETNAMESE SHAKING BEEF	137
09.	SICHUAN PEPPER BEEF NOODLES	138
10.	SPICY CUMIN BEEF	140
11.	FIVE-SPICE LAMB CUTLETS	141
12.	INDIAN LAMB KOFTA	142
13.	SPICY LAMB RACK	145
14.	TANDOORI LAMB CUTLETS	146

STEAK WITH MISO BUTTER

SERVES 4, READY IN 15 MINUTES

4 × 200 g scotch fillet steaks
1 tablespoon olive oil
sea salt

Miso butter
250 g unsalted butter, softened
3 tablespoons shiro miso*
¼ cup finely sliced spring onions

Miso butter is a handy little flavour-booster to have stored in your freezer. There will be far more than you need for this recipe so keep it in your freezer for up to two months and just slice off as much as you need each time.

My sides of choice for this dish are Wok-fried Asian Greens (page 174), roasted veggies or mashed potatoes.

STEP 1
To make the miso butter, place the butter, shiro miso and spring onions in a food processor and blitz until well combined. Spoon the butter onto a sheet of plastic wrap and roll up into a log. Pop it into the freezer to firm up a little while you tend to the steaks.

STEP 2
Rub the steaks with olive oil and generous sprinklings of sea salt. Heat a griddle pan or barbecue plate to high. Cook the steaks for 3–4 minutes on each side, or until cooked to your liking. Remove the steaks from the heat.

STEP 3
Take your miso butter out of the freezer and cut four thick slices (how thick depends on how naughty you want to be). Place butter slices on top of each warm steak and serve with your choice of sides.

* Shiro miso is a 'white' or 'sweet' miso, made from mainly rice and soybeans. It is available in the Asian section of most major supermarkets.

KOREAN STEAK SANDWICH

SERVES 4, READY IN 30 MINUTES

400 g beef scotch fillet or rump
   steaks, very thinly sliced
4 bread rolls, split in half
softened butter for spreading
½ cup roughly chopped fresh
   coriander

Marinade
¼ nashi pear, finely grated
3 garlic cloves, finely grated
2 teaspoons caster sugar
4 tablespoons light soy sauce
½ teaspoon sesame oil
½ cup finely sliced spring onions

Spicy mayo
3 tablespoons gochujang (Korean
   chilli paste)* (use sriracha chilli
   sauce as an alternative)
½ cup 'Kewpie' (Japanese)
   mayonnaise*

Quick pickle
1 small Lebanese cucumber,
   cut into thin rounds
1 small carrot, cut into fine
   strips using a julienne peeler
   or coarsely grated
2 teaspoons rice vinegar
2 teaspoons caster sugar

A good steak sambo is a joy to behold and this Korean-inspired version is
no exception. Adding nashi pear to the marinade helps to tenderise your
beef before it's cooked.

STEP 1
Preheat the oven grill to high.

STEP 2
Place the beef in a large bowl then add the marinade ingredients.
Mix to combine and set aside while you prepare everything else.

STEP 3
For the spicy mayo, mix the gochujang and 'Kewpie' (Japanese)
mayonnaise. Set aside for later.

STEP 4
To make the quick pickle, toss all the ingredients together and then
set aside.

STEP 5
Spread the cut sides of the rolls with butter and toast them under the
preheated oven grill for about a minute, until golden brown. Turn the oven
grill off but keep the rolls warm in the oven.

STEP 6
Heat a wok over high heat until smoking hot then add the beef and any
remaining marinade. Stir-fry for 2–3 minutes, until the beef is just cooked.
Remove the beef from the heat.

STEP 7
To assemble your steak sandwiches, spread the cut side of each roll
generously with spicy mayo. Place a small handful of pickled cucumber
and carrot on the bottom half of each roll then add some beef slices
and coriander and top with the remaining bread half.

* Gochujang (Korean chilli paste) is a
  spicy, smoky chilli paste found at
  most Asian grocers.

* 'Kewpie' (Japanese) mayonnaise is
  available in the Asian section of
  most major supermarkets.

SOY–GINGER EYE FILLET STEAKS

6 × 200 g beef eye fillet steaks
1 tablespoon vegetable oil
1 cup beef stock
3 whole star anise

Marinade
1 tablespoon finely grated
    fresh ginger
3 garlic cloves, finely chopped
4 tablespoons light soy sauce
2 teaspoons dark soy sauce
2 teaspoons sesame oil
¼ cup shaoxing (Chinese
    cooking wine)*
3 tablespoons honey

I'm a big fan of marinades that do their work quickly and efficiently. Just ten minutes is all the marinating your steaks need but up to a couple of hours is okay too. I'd be wary of leaving your steaks to soak any longer because soy sauce–based marinades can impart too much of a salty flavour if left for too long.

Your marinade also doubles as the base for a beefy, gingery sauce. So all you need is some creamy mash or a green salad and you're good to go.

STEP 1
In a large bowl, combine the steaks and the marinade ingredients. Let the flavours infuse for about 10 minutes.

STEP 2
Brush a large, non-stick frying pan with the vegetable oil and place over high heat. Remove the beef from the marinade (reserving the remaining liquid) and cook the steaks for about 4 minutes on each side (for medium–rare), or until cooked to your liking.

STEP 3
Transfer the steaks to a plate to rest for 5 minutes.

STEP 4
Meanwhile, add the stock, the reserved marinade and the star anise to the frying pan that you browned the beef in and bring to the boil over medium–high heat. Simmer for 5 minutes, or until the liquid has thickened slightly. Remove the star anise with a slotted spoon.

STEP 5
Serve the steaks with the warm sauce and your choice of sides.

* Shaoxing is a Chinese wine made from fermented rice. Find it at your Asian grocer and some major supermarkets.

VIETNAMESE BEEF NOODLE SALAD

SERVES 4, READY IN 30 MINUTES

300 g rump steak, very thinly
  sliced
200 g dried rice vermicelli
  noodles
1 small Lebanese cucumber,
  deseeded and thinly sliced on
  the diagonal
1 small carrot, cut into fine
  strips using a julienne peeler or
  coarsely grated
2 tablespoons vegetable oil
½ cup Thai basil leaves
½ cup mint leaves
1 cup bean shoots
½ cup fried shallots*

Marinade

1 teaspoon black peppercorns
1 lemongrass stalk, white part
  only, bruised and sliced
3 garlic cloves
1 tablespoon fish sauce
1 teaspoon caster sugar

Sauce

1 tablespoon rice vinegar
¼ cup fish sauce
2 tablespoons caster sugar

The streets of Hanoi are hot, steamy and punctuated by the roar of a never-ending stream of motorbikes. I'd been walking and sweltering for more than two hours, trying to find a particularly well-known hole-in-the-wall joint famous for its *bun bo nam bo*, a kind of Vietnamese beef noodle salad. Just as I was thinking of giving up, I found it. Tucked into a side street, it was more alleyway than restaurant, but I was rewarded with a bowlful of juicy, marinated strips of beef served on noodles piled high with crispy fried shallots.

STEP 1

To make the marinade, use a mortar and pestle to pound the peppercorns, lemongrass and garlic to a rough paste. Transfer the paste to a bowl and stir through the fish sauce and caster sugar. Add the beef and mix to combine. Set aside to marinate while you prepare the rest of the salad ingredients.

STEP 2

Cook the vermicelli noodles in boiling water for 2 minutes, or until tender. Drain and rinse under running water to cool. Use scissors to cut the noodles into shorter lengths. Divide between four serving bowls and top with the cucumber and carrot.

STEP 3

In a small bowl, whisk the sauce ingredients together. Set aside until ready to use.

STEP 4

Heat the vegetable oil in a wok over high heat. Add the beef and stir-fry for 2–3 minutes, until almost cooked. Add the sauce mixture and simmer for a minute.

STEP 5

Remove from the heat and divide the beef and sauce mixture between the noodle bowls. Top with the basil, mint, bean shoots and fried shallots. Serve warm.

* Jars or packets of ready-made fried
  shallots or onions can be bought from the
  Asian aisle of most supermarkets or an
  Asian grocer.

ROAST PEPPER BEEF WITH PONZU

4 tablespoons black peppercorns

2 teaspoons coriander seeds

2 teaspoons sea salt

2 beef eye fillet steaks (about 500 g each)

1 tablespoon vegetable oil

1 handful (about 50 g) rocket leaves to serve

Ponzu

2 tablespoons finely sliced spring onion

2 tablespoons Japanese soy sauce

1 tablespoon rice vinegar

finely grated zest of 1 lemon

2 tablespoons lemon juice

1 tablespoon honey

1 teaspoon finely grated fresh ginger

This is my Japanese-inspired version of roast beef. Ponzu is a traditional Japanese sauce with a tart, citrussy flavour. It pairs beautifully with any grilled or roasted meats and is particularly lovely with this peppery, coriander-crusted beef. I like to serve this dish with roasted vegetables, mashed potatoes or even just a simple green salad.

STEP 1

Preheat the oven to 200°C. Line a baking tray with foil.

STEP 2

Place the peppercorns, coriander seeds and salt in a mortar and use a pestle to coarsely crush. Transfer to a large plate. Roll each beef fillet in the pepper mixture until evenly coated.

STEP 3

Place a large non-stick frying pan over high heat and brush with vegetable oil. Add the beef fillets and cook, turning occasionally, for 6 minutes, until browned. Transfer the beef fillets to the lined baking tray and roast in your preheated oven for 15 minutes (for medium–rare), or until cooked to your liking. Remove the beef fillets from the oven and rest for 2 minutes.

STEP 4

While your beef is roasting, whisk the ponzu ingredients together and pour into a serving bowl.

STEP 5

Cut the beef into roughly 2 cm-thick slices and serve with rocket leaves and the ponzu.

BEEF PHO

SERVES 4, READY IN 30 MINUTES

400 g dried rice stick noodles
½ brown onion, halved and
   thinly sliced
250 g beef fillet steak

Broth

1 teaspoon vegetable oil
1 brown onion, roughly chopped
5 cm piece ginger, peeled
   and sliced
5 garlic cloves, roughly chopped
3 whole star anise
2 cinnamon sticks
2 litres beef stock
½ cup fish sauce
3 tablespoons light soy sauce
2 teaspoons white sugar

Table condiments

hoisin sauce
sambal oelek*
bean shoots
Thai basil leaves
lemon wedges
long red chillies, finely sliced

I am a noodle soup devotee from way back. I love the humble noodle soup in all its glorious variations – Singaporean laksa, Thai pork, Chinese wonton, Japanese ramen and, of course, one of my absolute favourites, the Vietnamese pho.

Traditionally, the broth would be left to simmer away for hours on end. My express version obviously has a lighter flavour than the traditional but it still delivers a beefy, savoury soup with just a hint of star anise – and all in record time.

STEP 1

To make the broth, heat the vegetable oil in a large pot over medium–high heat. Add the onion, ginger, garlic, star anise and cinnamon sticks. Cook, stirring every so often, for 3–4 minutes, or until the onion has softened. Add the beef stock, fish sauce, soy sauce and sugar. Bring to the boil then turn down the heat to medium and simmer for 20 minutes.

STEP 2

While your broth is simmering away, cook the noodles according to the packet instructions. Drain and rinse under running water to cool. Divide between four serving bowls and top with the onion slices.

STEP 3

Now it's time to get all your table condiments in order. Place the hoisin and sambal oelek in little bowls so people can add their own sauces to taste. Place a pile of bean shoots, basil leaves, lemon wedges and chillies on a platter. These, too, are to be picked, squeezed or sprinkled over soup bowls to taste.

STEP 4

Just before your broth is done, slice the beef into ever-so-thin slivers and drape them over the noodles and onion. Carefully strain the broth into a clean saucepan and place back on high heat until it just comes back to a simmer. Ladle the hot broth over the beef so that it just cooks. Serve with the range of table condiments.

* Sambal oelek is a spicy paste made from fresh red chillies and can be found in the Asian aisle of some supermarkets or at any Asian grocer.

THAI BEEF SALAD

2 × 200 g rump or sirloin steaks

2 teaspoons vegetable oil

½ teaspoon sea salt

½ small red onion, thinly sliced

1 small Lebanese cucumber, halved lengthways, deseeded and sliced on the diagonal

½ cup mint leaves

3 spring onions, trimmed and cut into 4 cm batons

½ cup roughly chopped fresh coriander

2 teaspoons chilli flakes (or to taste)

Dressing

3 tablespoons fish sauce

1 tablespoon white sugar

2 tablespoons lime juice

My mum's Thai beef salad was a staple weeknight dinner for me as a child. Traditionally, it's a super spicy salad and I can remember many burning-mouth episodes whenever my mum dished it up. But, of course, without a Thai mother wielding the chilli flakes, you can add as little or as much as you like.

Traditionally this would be served warm with rice (see my Steamed Jasmine Rice on page 178) but if you're serving it on its own as a main course you may want to double the quantities.

STEP 1
Rub the steaks with the vegetable oil and sprinkle with the sea salt.

STEP 2
Heat a griddle pan or non-stick frying pan over high heat and cook the steaks for 2–3 minutes on each side, until medium–rare. Remove from the heat and rest for 3 minutes.

STEP 3
To make the dressing, whisk the ingredients together in a small bowl.

STEP 4
In a large bowl, place the red onion, cucumber, mint, spring onions and coriander.

STEP 5
Slice the rested beef into very thin strips and add to the red onion mixture. Pour over the dressing and sprinkle with chilli flakes. Toss to combine and serve.

VIETNAMESE SHAKING BEEF

SERVES 4, READY IN 15 MINUTES

500 g scotch fillet or sirloin
steaks, thinly sliced
1 tablespoon vegetable oil
2 handfuls (about 100 g)
watercress
juice of 1 lime

Marinade
2 tablespoons oyster sauce
2 teaspoons fish sauce
2 garlic cloves, finely chopped
1 teaspoon white sugar
1 teaspoon ground black pepper

Pickled red onion
½ small red onion, finely sliced
1 tablespoon rice vinegar
1 teaspoon white sugar

In Vietnam this dish is called 'bo luc lac', which translates literally as 'beef shaking'. The name always makes me smile because it conjures up images of seared slices of beef quivering on the plate. In fact, 'luc lac' refers to the 'shaking' that happens in the wok. Whether it's quivering or not quivering, this is one mighty tasty treatment for beef and the pickled red onion adds such a beautiful tang to the whole dish. I like to serve it with Steamed Jasmine Rice (page 178).

STEP 1
Make the marinade by mixing the ingredients together in a large bowl. Add the beef and mix to combine.

STEP 2
For the pickled red onion, toss the ingredients together and set aside.

STEP 3
Heat the vegetable oil in a wok over high heat. When the wok is smoking hot, add the beef and stir-fry for 2–3 minutes, until just cooked.

STEP 4
Place the warm beef, the watercress and lime juice in a large bowl. Add the drained pickled red onion slices. Toss gently until just combined. Serve warm.

SICHUAN PEPPER BEEF NOODLES

SERVES 4, READY IN 25 MINUTES

270 g (1 packet) dried udon
   noodles
2 teaspoons Sichuan
   peppercorns*
1 tablespoon vegetable oil
1 tablespoon sesame oil
1 brown onion, halved and
   thinly sliced
1 long red chilli, finely chopped
3 garlic cloves, finely chopped
500 g beef mince
2 tablespoons light soy sauce
3 tablespoons oyster sauce
3 spring onions, trimmed and
   cut into 2 cm batons
chilli flakes to serve

I'm always on the lookout for inspiring mince recipes and this one really is a cracker. The tingling sensation from the Sichuan peppercorns makes the dish. Pork, chicken or turkey mince work equally well here.

STEP 1

Cook the udon noodles according to the packet instructions. Drain and rinse under running water to cool.

STEP 2

While your noodles are cooking, place the Sichuan peppercorns in a dry frying pan over medium–high heat and cook, shaking the pan often, for about a minute or until the pan is just starting to smoke. Transfer the peppercorns to a mortar and use a pestle to grind them to a fine powder.

STEP 3

When your noodles are cooked and ready to go, heat the vegetable and sesame oils in a wok over high heat. Add the onion, chilli and garlic and stir-fry for about a minute. Add the Sichuan pepper powder and beef and stir-fry for 2–3 minutes, until the beef is just cooked. Add the cooked noodles, soy sauce and oyster sauce and toss until all the ingredients are well combined. Remove from the heat and toss through the spring onions. Sprinkle with as many pinches of chilli flakes as you can handle and serve warm.

* Sichuan peppercorns are available in the spice section of some major supermarkets or at your Asian grocer.

SPICY CUMIN BEEF

SERVES 4, READY IN 15 MINUTES

600 g steak (sirloin, porterhouse or scotch are fine), very thinly sliced

2 tablespoons vegetable oil

1 tablespoon finely grated fresh ginger

3 garlic cloves, finely chopped

2 teaspoons whole cumin seeds

8 whole dried long red chillies (or to taste)

3 spring onions, trimmed and cut into 2 cm batons

Marinade

1 tablespoon shaoxing (Chinese cooking wine)*

1 tablespoon light soy sauce

1 teaspoon ground cumin

2 teaspoons cornflour

Sauce

2 tablespoons light soy sauce

1 tablespoon shaoxing (Chinese cooking wine)*

1 teaspoon sriracha chilli sauce*

Cumin is not a spice you would typically associate with Chinese food but in China's Hunan province it's a more common ingredient. The combination of dried red chillies and cumin seeds here creates a magically spicy flavour. Just be ready when you're frying off those chillies – open up your windows and prepare to cough! Dried long red chillies are typically not as spicy as the small dried bird's eye chillies; use fewer chillies if you're worried about the heat. If you like things super hot, chop up a couple of the dried chillies before adding them.

This dish packs quite a punch with the spices and chilli heat so I like to serve it with plain rice and/or some steamed Asian greens.

STEP 1

In a large bowl, combine the steak with the marinade ingredients.

STEP 2

In a separate bowl, whisk the sauce ingredients together.

STEP 3

Heat the vegetable oil in a wok over high heat. Add the ginger, garlic, cumin seeds and chillies. Toss everything about in the wok for about 30 seconds (careful of those chilli fumes!). Add the marinated beef and stir-fry for 2–3 minutes, until almost cooked. Pour in the sauce mixture and stir-fry for another 30 seconds. Remove from the heat and toss through the spring onions. Serve with rice and/or Asian greens.

* Shaoxing is a Chinese wine made from fermented rice. Find it at your Asian grocer and some major supermarkets.

* Sriracha chilli sauce is a spicy, tangy chilli condiment. Find it in the Asian or sauce aisle of most supermarkets.

FIVE-SPICE LAMB CUTLETS

12 Frenched lamb cutlets
1 tablespoon sesame oil
1 teaspoon Chinese five-spice*
1 teaspoon sea salt

Hoisin glaze
¼ cup hoisin sauce
¼ cup beef stock

There are two schools of thought when it comes to meat bones and table manners – fingers or no fingers. I'm firmly in the fingers corner, especially when it comes to lamb cutlets. The best bits of lamb are firmly attached to the bone and there's no getting to them without a firm grip and tenacious gnawing.

The hoisin glaze in this recipe is a brilliant sauce for any kind of red meat and is especially good for barbecued or pan-fried steaks. I love to serve these juicy cutlets with a good dollop of mashed potato or pumpkin to soak up the sticky glaze and a nice crispy green salad for crunch.

STEP 1
Preheat the oven grill to high. Line a baking tray with foil.

STEP 2
Combine the lamb cutlets, sesame oil, Chinese five-spice and sea salt in a large bowl.

STEP 3
Spread the cutlets out on the lined baking tray. Place under the preheated grill and cook for 3 minutes, then turn over and cook for a further 3 minutes (for medium), or until cooked to your liking. Remove from the oven and rest for 3 minutes.

STEP 4
While your lamb is cooking, place the hoisin sauce and beef stock in a small saucepan over high heat and simmer for 5 minutes, until the sauce thickens slightly.

STEP 5
Serve the cutlets with the hoisin glaze and your choice of sides.

* Chinese five-spice is available in the spice
section of most major supermarkets.

INDIAN LAMB KOFTA

vegetable oil or olive oil spray
mint leaves to serve
lemon wedges to serve

Lamb kofta
2 eschallots, roughly chopped
3 garlic cloves, roughly chopped
500 g lamb mince
1 egg
2 heaped tablespoons finely
  chopped currants
½ cup panko breadcrumbs*
3 teaspoons ground cumin
2 teaspoons ground coriander
¼ teaspoon turmeric
¼ cup roughly chopped fresh
  coriander
1 teaspoon sea salt
mint leaves to serve
lemon wedges to serve

Spiced yoghurt sauce
1 cup thick natural yoghurt
1 small garlic clove
1 cup mint leaves
2 tablespoons lemon juice
1 teaspoon garam masala

These spiced kofta are great to freeze for later. They are good in lunchboxes, or try stuffing them into pita bread with lettuce, tomato and dollops of yoghurt sauce. My Spiced Indian Rice (page 184) is also a tasty accompaniment.

STEP 1
Preheat the oven to 200°C. Line a baking tray with foil and lightly brush or spray with oil. Place the lined baking tray in your oven to preheat.

STEP 2
To make the spiced yoghurt sauce, place all the ingredients in the bowl of a food processor and whizz until smooth. Empty the sauce into a serving bowl.

STEP 3
For the lamb kofta, place all the ingredients in the same food processor (don't worry about cleaning it) and pulse until well combined. Shape into 12 small oval patties and place on the preheated oven tray. Cook in the oven for 16 minutes (turning after about 8 minutes), or until just cooked through.

STEP 4
Serve the kofta with a sprinkling of mint leaves, lemon wedges and the spiced yoghurt sauce.

* Panko is a type of large, flaky breadcrumb that becomes super crispy when fried and is available at most major supermarkets or any Asian grocer..

SPICY LAMB RACK

SERVES 4, READY IN 30 MINUTES

4 x 3-cutlet Frenched lamb racks

Spice paste

1 tablespoon finely grated fresh
  ginger
3 garlic cloves, finely grated
3 tablespoons vegetable oil
2 teaspoons garam masala
½ teaspoon turmeric
2 teaspoons cumin seeds
1 teaspoon chilli flakes
  (or to taste)
1 teaspoon sea salt
2 tablespoons finely chopped
  fresh coriander

Mint yoghurt

¼ cup thick natural yoghurt
2 tablespoons finely chopped
  mint leaves

The spice paste in this recipe creates a beautiful crust on the lamb as it cooks. This is a lovely dinner party dish and can be served with creamy mashed potatoes, Bombay Potatoes (page 161) or Spiced Indian Rice (page 184).

STEP 1
Preheat the oven to 200°C. Line a baking tray with foil.

STEP 2
Combine the spice paste ingredients in a large bowl. Place the lamb racks in the bowl and use your hands to toss them with the spice paste until they are well coated.

STEP 3
Heat a large non-stick frying pan over medium–high heat and sear the lamb racks for about 2 minutes, turning them so that they brown evenly. Transfer the lamb to the lined baking tray and roast in the oven for 15 minutes (for medium), or until cooked to your liking. Allow to rest for 3 minutes.

STEP 4
In the meantime, mix together the ingredients for the mint yoghurt and set aside until ready to serve.

STEP 5
Serve the cutlets with the mint yoghurt and your choice of sides.

TANDOORI LAMB CUTLETS

SERVES 4, READY IN 20 MINUTES

¼ cup tandoori paste

2 tablespoons thick natural
  yoghurt

16 Frenched lamb cutlets

1 tablespoon vegetable oil

2 tablespoons roughly chopped
  fresh coriander to serve

Pomegranate raita

1 cup thick natural yoghurt

½ cup pomegranate seeds*

1 long green chilli, deseeded and
  finely chopped

2 tablespoons roughly chopped
  fresh coriander

1 tablespoon lemon juice

½ teaspoon ground cumin

I adore this pomegranate raita studded with little ruby-red jewels. Use this raita with any curry dish for something a little different from the usual cucumber and mint version. My Bombay Potatoes (page 161) or Spiced Indian Rice (page 184) make good companions for this lamb.

STEP 1

In a large bowl, combine the tandoori paste and yoghurt. Add the lamb cutlets and toss well to coat. Set aside while you make your raita.

STEP 2

For the pomegranate raita, place the ingredients in a bowl, reserving 1–2 tablespoons of pomegranate seeds to garnish. Mix until well combined. Spoon the raita into a serving bowl and set aside in the fridge until ready to serve.

STEP 3

Heat a barbecue plate or large griddle pan over medium–high heat. Lightly brush the plate or pan with the vegetable oil and cook the cutlets for about 2–3 minutes on each side (for medium–rare), or until done to your liking.

STEP 5

Serve the lamb with the pomegranate raita, a sprinkling of fresh coriander and the reserved pomegranate seeds.

* To get the seeds out of a pomegranate, cut the fruit into quarters. Hold a quarter, cut-side down, in the palm of your hand and hit the back of the fruit with a wooden spoon. Be careful not to miss!

VEGGIES & EGGS

01.	CURRY-SPICED CORN FRITTERS	150
02.	THAI MUSHROOM SALAD	153
03.	VEGETABLE CURRY WITH PESHWARI NAAN	154
04.	FRIED EGGS WITH CRAZY SAUCE	156
05.	MISO MUSHROOM SPAGHETTI	158
06.	BOMBAY POTATOES	161
07.	CRISPY EGG TOFU	162
08.	COCONUT-PUMPKIN SOUP	164
09.	MASALA CHICKPEAS & SPINACH	165
10.	SWEET CHILLI-COCONUT COLESLAW	167
11.	RED POTATO SALAD	168
12.	ASIAN VEGETABLE OMELETTE	170
13.	CHILLI EGGPLANT	173
14.	WOK-FRIED ASIAN GREENS	174

CURRY-SPICED CORN FRITTERS

250 g cherry tomatoes
1 tablespoon vegetable oil,
  plus extra for shallow-frying
1 teaspoon ground cumin
sea salt
½ cup self-raising flour
2 eggs
1 tablespoon curry powder
2 cups fresh corn kernels (3 large
  corn cobs should do it)

Mint and coriander yoghurt

1 cup roughly chopped fresh
  coriander
½ cup mint leaves
1 small garlic clove
2 tablespoons lemon juice
¾ cup thick natural yoghurt

Ooooh, these are tasty little critters. Make them for breakfast, lunch or a light supper. You can use thawed frozen corn kernels instead of fresh if that's easier.

STEP 1

Preheat the oven to 200°C.

STEP 2

In a non-stick baking tray, toss the cherry tomatoes with 1 tablespoon of vegetable oil, the cumin and a generous pinch of sea salt. Roast for 20 minutes, until the tomatoes are soft. Keep warm in the oven until ready to serve.

STEP 3

While your tomatoes are roasting, place all the ingredients for the mint and coriander yoghurt in a food processor and whizz until smooth. Transfer to a bowl.

STEP 4

In the same food processor bowl (don't bother washing it), place the self-raising flour, eggs, curry powder, 1 cup of the corn kernels and 1 teaspoon of sea salt. Whizz until you have a well-combined batter. Pour out into a mixing bowl and stir through the remaining corn kernels.

STEP 5

Pour enough vegetable oil into a large non-stick frying pan to just cover the base. Place the pan over medium–high heat. When hot, pour in heaped tablespoons of the corn batter, spreading the mixture out slightly with the back of a spoon. Fit as many fritters as you can into the pan and cook for about 2 minutes on each side, or until golden brown. Keep the cooked fritters warm in the oven while you cook the remaining batter.

STEP 6

Serve the fritters with generous dollops of mint and coriander yoghurt and the roasted cumin tomatoes.

THAI MUSHROOM SALAD

2 tablespoons raw rice

2 tablespoons vegetable oil

600 g mixed Asian mushrooms
  such as enoki, shimeji, king
  brown, oyster and shiitake,
  with larger mushrooms cut
  into bite-sized pieces

1 eschallot, thinly sliced

2 teaspoons chilli flakes
  (or to taste)

3 tablespoons fish sauce

3 tablespoons lime juice

1 teaspoon sugar

½ cup mint leaves

¼ cup roughly chopped fresh
  coriander

2 spring onions, cut into
  2 cm batons

Traditionally, 'laab' salad is a super spicy Thai dish made from minced meat but my mum's mushroom version is equally mouthwatering. It's notoriously hard to get a recipe out of my mum because her style of cooking is purely instinctive. Her Thai cooking always involves tasting, adjusting and seasoning, with every addition quantified by taste, not by a measuring spoon.

So channel your inner Thai mamma here and aim to balance those spicy, sweet, sour and salty flavours with your chilli, sugar, lime juice and fish sauce. Think of these ingredients as you would salt and pepper.

Serve with Steamed Jasmine Rice (page 178) and/or lettuce leaves to scoop up the bundles of spicy mushroom salad.

STEP 1

Cook the raw rice in a dry frying pan over high heat, shaking the pan often, for 4 minutes, or until golden brown. Then use a mortar and pestle to grind the toasted rice to a fine powder.

STEP 2

Heat the vegetable oil in a wok over high heat. Add the mushrooms and stir-fry for 2–3 minutes, or until the mushrooms just start to collapse. Remove the wok from the heat and toss through the ground roasted rice, eschallot, chilli flakes, fish sauce, lime juice, sugar, mint, coriander and spring onions. Now this is where your tastebuds need to do some work. Taste your salad and add more chilli, fish sauce, lime juice and sugar as you please.

STEP 3

Pile onto a plate and serve.

VEGETABLE CURRY WITH PESHWARI NAAN

SERVES 4, READY IN 30 MINUTES

1 brown onion, roughly chopped

4 garlic cloves, roughly chopped

1 tablespoon roughly chopped fresh ginger

3 tablespoons vegetable oil

3 teaspoons ground coriander

1 teaspoon ground cumin

½ teaspoon turmeric

¼ teaspoon chilli powder (or to taste)

1 cup vegetable stock

400 g can crushed tomatoes

200 g butternut pumpkin, peeled and cut into rough 2 cm cubes

200 g (about ¼ small) cauliflower, cut into small florets

200 g (about ½ large) eggplant, cut into rough 2 cm cubes

2 teaspoons garam masala

2 tablespoons thick natural yoghurt, lightly whisked, plus extra to serve

roughly chopped fresh coriander to serve

Peshwari naan

4 store-bought naan breads

butter for spreading

½ cup desiccated coconut

¼ cup almond flakes

¼ cup raisins

Peshwari naan is a traditional Indian flatbread stuffed with nuts, coconut and dried fruit. My cheat's peshwari naan takes advantage of the pre-made naan breads that are now readily available in supermarkets. Simply stuff with coconut, almonds, raisins and heat. As with all curries, this one tastes even better the next day, so save the leftovers for tomorrow's lunch.

STEP 1
Preheat the oven to 180°C. Line a baking tray with foil.

STEP 2
Place the onion, garlic and ginger in the bowl of a food processor and pulse until finely chopped.

STEP 3
Heat the vegetable oil in a saucepan over medium–high heat and cook the onion mixture for 3 minutes, or until softened. Add the coriander, cumin, turmeric and chilli powder and cook, stirring, for another minute. Add the vegetable stock, tomatoes, pumpkin, cauliflower and eggplant. Cover with a lid and simmer for 15 minutes, or until the vegetables are tender. Remove from the heat and stir through the garam masala and yoghurt.

STEP 4
While your curry is cooking, split the naan breads in half. Spread each cut side of naan with butter. Combine the coconut, almonds and raisins in a bowl, then sprinkle the mixture onto the bottom halves of each naan bread. Top with the remaining slices of naan bread (buttered-side down) and push down gently. Place the stuffed naan on the baking tray and warm in the oven for 5 minutes. Cut each naan into large wedges.

STEP 5
Serve the curry with a sprinkling of coriander, extra yoghurt and the warm naan bread wedges.

FRIED EGGS WITH CRAZY SAUCE

vegetable oil for shallow-frying
4 eggs
2 garlic cloves, finely chopped
1 long red chilli, finely chopped
2 tablespoons oyster sauce
1 tablespoon finely sliced
spring onion
1 tablespoon finely chopped
fresh coriander
1 tablespoon fried shallots*

So simple but crazy good (hence the name). A bowl of Steamed Jasmine Rice (page 178) and a couple of these make dinner a breeze.

STEP 1

Heat 1 cm of vegetable oil in a large non-stick frying pan over high heat. When the oil is hot, crack in your eggs. Cook the eggs for about a minute (for runny eggs), spooning the hot oil over the tops of the eggs to help them cook. Scoop the cooked eggs out onto a serving platter.

STEP 2

Pour off all but 2 tablespoons of the oil from the pan. Place the pan back over the heat and add the garlic and chilli. Stir-fry for about 30 seconds, until the garlic starts to brown. Add the oyster sauce and 1 tablespoon of water. Stir to combine, then remove from the heat.

STEP 3

Spoon the sauce over the eggs. Sprinkle over the spring onion, coriander and fried shallots and serve.

* Jars or packets of ready-made fried shallots or onions can be bought from the Asian aisle of most supermarkets or an Asian grocer.

MISO MUSHROOM SPAGHETTI

SERVES 2, READY IN 20 MINUTES

200 g dried spaghetti
50 g unsalted butter
3 garlic cloves, finely chopped
200 g mixed mushrooms such
   as Swiss brown, shiitake,
   oyster or shimeji, cut into
   rough chunks
3 tablespoons shiro miso*
½ cup finely sliced spring onions
¼ cup grated parmesan, plus
   extra to serve (optional)

Miso is a traditional Japanese seasoning paste best known as the main ingredient in 'miso soup'. There are many different varieties but the most common types available are 'red' and 'white' miso. 'White' (also called 'shiro miso') is the easiest to get hold of in major supermarkets and is lighter and sweeter than its red miso cousin.

I like to think of miso as more than just an ingredient for a soothing broth (although I do *love* miso soup). Using it in this spaghetti dish accentuates the savoury flavour of the mushrooms and adds a toasty, nuttiness to the sauce.

STEP 1
Cook the spaghetti in boiling salted water until al dente.

STEP 2
While your pasta is cooking, heat the butter in a large, deep frying pan over medium–high heat. When the butter starts to foam, throw in your garlic and mushrooms. Toss and cook for about 2 minutes.

STEP 3
Add the shiro miso and 1 cup of water to the mushrooms. Swirl around until the miso dissolves and then simmer gently, uncovered, for about 5 minutes to thicken the sauce slightly.

STEP 4
Drain the pasta and toss through the mushroom sauce, together with the spring onions and parmesan.

STEP 5
Pile into bowls and serve with extra parmesan, if desired.

* Shiro miso is a 'white' or 'sweet' miso, made from mainly rice and soybeans. It is available in the Asian section of most major supermarkets.

BOMBAY POTATOES

1 kg potatoes, cut into rough
  2 cm cubes (peeled or unpeeled
  – it's up to you!)
2 tablespoons vegetable oil
2 brown onions, halved and
  thinly sliced
2 teaspoons brown mustard
  seeds
1 teaspoon turmeric
2 teaspoons garam masala
2 teaspoons sea salt
3 tablespoons roughly chopped
  fresh coriander

Sweet, golden onions, creamy potato and fragrant spices make this more than just a side dish. You can serve it alongside an Indian curry or on its own with rice, naan bread and a dollop of natural yoghurt.

STEP 1

Cook the potatoes in boiling water for 20 minutes, or until just tender but still slightly firm in the middle.

STEP 2

While your potatoes are cooking, heat the oil in a large frying pan or wok over medium–high heat and cook the onions for 10–12 minutes. They should be dark golden and soft by the time you're done. Then add the mustard seeds, turmeric and garam masala. Cook, stirring, for about a minute, or until the mustard seeds start to pop. Remove from the heat until your potatoes are done.

STEP 3

When your potatoes are cooked, drain them and return your onion mixture to the heat. Add the potatoes and sea salt to the onion mixture and toss until well combined. Remove from the heat, sprinkle with fresh coriander and serve.

CRISPY EGG TOFU

SERVES 4 AS A SHARED STARTER, READY IN 30 MINUTES

¼ cup cornflour
250 g egg tofu*
vegetable oil for shallow-frying
¼ cup finely sliced spring onions

Chilli sauce
2 long red chillies, roughly
  chopped
3 eschallots, roughly chopped
4 garlic cloves, roughly chopped
3 cm piece ginger, peeled and
  roughly chopped
3 tablespoons vegetable oil
4 tablespoons light soy sauce
1 tablespoon Chinese black
  vinegar*

Egg tofu is the richer, silkier cousin of regular tofu. You'll find egg tofu in squishy clear tubes in the fridge section of your Asian grocer. It's easy to prepare because you just cut the end off the tube, gently ease out the tofu and slice it into rounds that look like fat scallops.

You need gentle hands to slice, dip and fry these little rounds of goodness but it's well worth the effort. These are a favourite in my house, even among hard-core tofu disbelievers.

STEP 1
To make the chilli sauce, combine the chillies, eschallots, garlic and ginger in a food processor and pulse until finely chopped (you could also do this by hand).

STEP 2
Now heat the oil in a small saucepan over medium–high heat and cook the chilli mixture for 5 minutes, or until soft. Add the soy sauce and black vinegar and cook, stirring, for another minute. Remove from the heat.

STEP 3
Spread the cornflour out onto a large plate and set aside for later.

STEP 4
Slice one end off the tofu tube and carefully ease out the tofu, keeping it in one whole piece. Slice into rounds 2 cm thick.

STEP 5
Heat a 1 cm depth of vegetable oil in a large non-stick frying pan over medium–high heat. Dip each round of tofu into the cornflour on both sides and carefully place into the hot oil. Don't overcrowd the pan – fry the tofu rounds in batches if necessary. Cook the tofu for 2 minutes on each side, or until golden brown. Drain on paper towel.

STEP 6
Arrange the tofu rounds on a serving plate and top each with a heaped teaspoon of the chilli sauce and a sprinkling of spring onions. Serve immediately.

* Egg tofu is made by adding eggs to the soy milk before it has set. It's available in the fridge section of Asian grocers.

* Chinese black vinegar is a dark, complex vinegar that you can find at your Asian grocer.

COCONUT-PUMPKIN SOUP

1 brown onion, peeled and
 quartered
3 garlic cloves, peeled
4 cm piece ginger, peeled
1 tablespoon vegetable oil
¼ teaspoon turmeric
1 kg pumpkin, peeled and cut
 into rough 2 cm cubes
2 cups vegetable stock
2 cups coconut milk
3 tablespoons fish sauce
2 tablespoons honey
sour cream to serve
freshly ground black pepper

I'm a pumpkin soup hoarder. I've always got a batch of creamy pumpkin goodness stored in my freezer for emergencies. If I'm making this for dinner, I like to have big chunks of buttered sourdough toast on hand for dunking.

STEP 1

Pulse the onion, garlic and ginger in a food processor until roughly chopped (you could also do this by hand).

STEP 2

Heat the oil in a large stockpot over medium–high heat. Add the onion mixture and turmeric and cook for 5 minutes, until the vegetables are soft. Add the pumpkin, vegetable stock, coconut milk, fish sauce and honey. Cover with a lid and simmer for 20 minutes, or until the pumpkin is soft. Remove from the heat.

STEP 3

Use a handheld blender or food processor (in which case, let the soup cool a little first) to blitz the soup until smooth.

STEP 4

Ladle the soup into bowls and top with a dollop of sour cream and a generous grinding of pepper.

MASALA CHICKPEAS & SPINACH

2 tablespoons ghee or vegetable oil

1 brown onion, halved and thinly sliced

2 garlic cloves, finely chopped

1 tablespoon finely grated fresh ginger

1 tablespoon garam masala

1 teaspoon brown mustard seeds

½ teaspoon turmeric

½ teaspoon chilli powder (or to taste)

1 tablespoon tomato paste

1 tomato, finely chopped

2 x 400 g cans chickpeas, drained and rinsed

1 small handful (about 50 g) baby spinach leaves

thick natural yoghurt to serve (optional)

'Chana masala' is a spicy Indian chickpea dish. My version makes use of canned chickpeas to cut out the soaking and simmering usually required. Any leftovers make a great cold lunch the next day.

STEP 1

Heat the ghee or vegetable oil in a large saucepan over medium–high heat and cook the onion for at least 3–4 minutes, or until soft. Add the garlic and ginger and cook for another minute. Add the garam masala, mustard seeds, turmeric and chilli powder and cook for another minute. Stir through the tomato paste, tomato and ½ cup of water. Cover with a lid and simmer on low for 5 minutes.

STEP 2

Remove the lid and stir through the chickpeas and baby spinach. Cover and cook on low for another 2–3 minutes, until the spinach has wilted.

STEP 3

Serve with a dollop of yoghurt if desired.

SWEET CHILLI–COCONUT COLESLAW

SERVES 6, READY IN 15 MINUTES

4 cups finely shredded wombok
2 cup finely shredded red
  cabbage
1 large carrot, cut into fine
  strips using a julienne peeler
  or coarsely grated
1 cup finely sliced spring onions
¼ cup roughly torn mint leaves

Sweet chilli–coconut dressing
1 cup sweet chilli sauce
½ cup coconut milk, lightly
  whisked
4 tablespoons lime juice

This coleslaw is just dying to make friends with a plate of barbecued sausages, lamb chops or grilled steaks.

STEP 1
Combine the ingredients for the sweet chilli–coconut dressing in a bowl.

STEP 2
In a separate large bowl, toss together the wombok, red cabbage, carrot, spring onions, mint leaves and sweet chilli–coconut dressing.

RED POTATO SALAD

400 g small baby potatoes,
   quartered
3 cups finely shredded red
   cabbage
¼ cup finely sliced spring onions
½ cup 'Kewpie' (Japanese)
   mayonnaise*
2 tablespoons lime juice

This simple salad makes a great side dish for grilled steaks, lamb chops or crumbed fish.

STEP 1
Place the potatoes in a saucepan and cover with water. Bring to the boil and simmer for 15–20 minutes, or until the potatoes are just cooked through.

STEP 2
Drain the potatoes and toss with the red cabbage, spring onions, mayonnaise and lime juice. Serve warm or at room temperature.

* 'Kewpie' (Japanese) mayonnaise
  is available in the Asian section of
  most major supermarkets.

ASIAN VEGETABLE OMELETTE

2 tablespoons oyster sauce

4 eggs

1 teaspoon fish sauce

freshly ground black pepper

1 tablespoon vegetable oil

1 long red chilli, finely sliced

Filling

1 tablespoon vegetable oil

3 garlic cloves, finely chopped

1 cup bean shoots

1 small carrot, cut into fine
   strips using a julienne peeler
   or coarsely grated

½ red capsicum, cut into
   fine strips

1 tablespoon fish sauce

2 tablespoons finely chopped
   fresh coriander

1 spring onion, trimmed and
   cut into 5 cm batons

freshly ground black pepper

When time is short, this is my go-to weeknight dinner. Any stir-fry vegetables can be used as a substitute here – snow peas, broccolini or mushrooms all work well.

STEP 1

Mix the oyster sauce with 1 teaspoon of water and set aside for later.

STEP 2

To make the filling, heat the vegetable oil in a frying pan or wok over high heat. Add the garlic and stir-fry for 30 seconds. Add the bean shoots, carrot and capsicum and stir-fry for another minute. Add the fish sauce and stir-fry for another minute to soften the carrot. Remove from the heat and toss through the coriander, spring onion and loads of freshly ground black pepper.

STEP 3

To make the omelette, whisk the eggs with the fish sauce, 1 tablespoon of water and generous grindings of black pepper.

STEP 4

Heat the vegetable oil in a 25 cm non-stick frying pan over medium–high heat. Add the egg mixture and use a spatula to draw the egg in towards the centre. Swirl the pan to allow the uncooked egg to run out towards the edge. Keep doing this until the omelette is almost set.

STEP 5

Spoon the vegetable mixture over one half of the omelette. Flip the empty side of the omelette over the vegetables and turn out onto a serving plate. Drizzle with spoonfuls of the oyster sauce mixture and sprinkle with chilli slices. Share between two.

CHILLI EGGPLANT

2 tablespoons vegetable oil

1 tablespoon sesame oil

3 garlic cloves, finely chopped

1 tablespoon finely grated fresh
ginger

1 long red chilli, finely sliced
on the diagonal

1 large eggplant (about 400 g),
cut into bite-sized pieces

3 tablespoons oyster sauce

1 teaspoon white sugar

¼ cup finely sliced spring onions

chilli flakes to serve

The beauty of the humble eggplant lies in its wonderful ability to soak up flavours like a sponge. I find that if your eggplant is young and fresh, the need to pre-salt it becomes unnecessary. But if your eggplant is not as fresh as you'd like and you're worried about it being bitter, toss the chopped pieces with a generous sprinkling of salt and sit them in a colander for 20 minutes. Rinse with cold water and squeeze out the excess liquid before cooking.

STEP 1

Heat the vegetable and sesame oils in a wok over high heat. Add the garlic, ginger and chilli and stir-fry for about half a minute. Add the eggplant and stir-fry for a minute. Stir through the oyster sauce, sugar and ¼ cup of water. Cover with a lid for 2 minutes, lifting the lid to toss everything around every so often. Remove the lid and keep stir-frying and tossing the eggplant around in the wok for about a minute, or until the eggplant is tender.

STEP 2

Remove from the heat and scatter over the spring onions. Sprinkle with chilli flakes to taste.

WOK-FRIED ASIAN GREENS

I've used Chinese broccoli and bok choy for this recipe but any green vegetable will do here … broccolini, green beans, pak choy and morning glory are some of my favourites.

2 bunches Chinese broccoli
  (about 500 g)*
1/3 cup oyster sauce
2 tablespoons light soy sauce
1/2 teaspoon white sugar
2 tablespoons vegetable oil
3 garlic cloves, finely sliced
1 long red chilli, finely sliced
4 small bunches bok choy,
  halved lengthways

STEP 1

Prepare the Chinese broccoli by slicing each bunch in half to separate stems from leaves. Slice the leaves into roughly 4 cm-wide strips and set aside. Slice the stems into roughly 3 cm-long pieces and set aside.

STEP 2

In a small bowl, mix the oyster sauce, soy sauce and white sugar until combined.

STEP 3

Heat the vegetable oil in a wok over high heat. Add the garlic and chilli and stir-fry for about 30 seconds. Add the Chinese broccoli stems and stir-fry for about 2 minutes. Now add the Chinese broccoli leaves, bok choy and oyster sauce mixture. Stir-fry for a further 2 minutes until the leaves have just wilted. Remove from the heat and serve.

* Chinese broccoli is also known as gai lan or Chinese kale. It has a thick, pale-green stem and dark-green leaves. You can find it at some major supermarkets or any Asian grocer.

RICE

01.	STEAMED JASMINE RICE	178

FRIED RICE 3 WAYS

02.	CHINESE SAUSAGE & EGG FRIED RICE	181
03.	THAI CHICKEN FRIED RICE	182
04.	NASI GORENG	182

05.	SPICED INDIAN RICE	184

CONGEE 3 WAYS

06.	PORK & MUSHROOM CONGEE	187
07.	FISH CONGEE	188
08.	CHICKEN & EGG CONGEE	188

STEAMED JASMINE RICE

2 cups jasmine rice

In Thailand jasmine rice is called *'hom mali'*, literally, the 'smell of jasmine flowers'. A good-quality Thai jasmine rice should release that fragrant floral aroma as it steams.

Different varieties of rice require different cooking times and amounts of water, so if you are using a regular long grain rice or basmati rice instead of Thai jasmine rice, it would be best to follow the packet instructions.

STEP 1

Place the rice and 3 cups of water in a saucepan over high heat. Bring to the boil, then reduce the heat to low, cover with a lid and cook for 6 minutes. Lift the lid and give the rice a stir to help prevent it sticking to the saucepan. Replace the lid and cook for a further 6 minutes, until all the water has been absorbed.

STEP 2

Remove from the heat and let the rice stand, covered, for 5 minutes. Just before serving, use a fork to fluff up the rice.

THINGS TO DO WITH YOUR STEAMED JASMINE RICE

✱ Make a double batch for dinner and keep leftovers to make fried rice the next night (see pages 181–2 for fried rice ideas).

✱ Add a few heaped spoonfuls of rice to an Asian stock-based soup instead of noodles. Try it with my Miso Chicken Noodle Soup (page 66) or Char Siu Pork Noodle Soup (page 118).

THAI CHICKEN & GINGER STIR-FRY (PAGE 86)

SLIGHTLY CHARRY CHAR SIU SALMON (PAGE 54)

CHAR SIU PORK (PAGE 96)

FRIED RICE

3 WAYS

I am an unashamed devotee of fried rice. Give me a bowl of fried rice and the possibility of having seconds or thirds and I'm a happy girl. Fried rice is no chorus-line sidekick for me; it's absolutely the star of my dinner show.

The best rice to use is leftover or day-old cooked rice because it's drier and easier to stir-fry than when freshly made. I always make more rice than I need for any weeknight dinner so that I've got leftovers to make fried rice the next day.

CHINESE SAUSAGE & EGG FRIED RICE

SERVES 4, READY IN 20 MINUTES

2 tablespoons vegetable oil
3 Chinese sausages (lap cheong)*, thinly sliced
3 garlic cloves, finely chopped
1 brown onion, halved and cut into thin wedges
200 g sliced Asian greens such as bok choy, Chinese broccoli or pak choy
4 cups cooked rice
4 tablespoons light soy sauce
¼ cup finely sliced spring onions
2 teaspoons sesame oil
freshly ground black pepper

Omelette
3 eggs
1 teaspoon light soy sauce
freshly ground black pepper
1 tablespoon vegetable oil

STEP 1
To make the omelette, whisk the eggs with the soy sauce, 1 tablespoon of water and a generous grinding of pepper.

STEP 2
Heat 1 tablespoon of vegetable oil in a wok over high heat. Pour in the eggs and use your spatula to push the egg mixture from the centre out to the edges. Once the egg is nearly set, flip it over and cook for another minute. Transfer the cooked egg to a chopping board and roughly slice.

STEP 3
Heat 2 tablespoons of vegetable oil in the same wok over high heat and add the Chinese sausage. Stir-fry for about a minute, or until the sausage starts to char at the edges. Add the garlic and onion and stir-fry for another minute. Add the Asian greens and cook for another minute. Now add your rice and the soy sauce. Toss until the ingredients are well combined. Remove from the heat and toss through the spring onions, sesame oil and generous grindings of pepper.

* Chinese sausages (lap cheong) are available in the Asian section of most major supermarkets or from an Asian grocer.

THAI CHICKEN FRIED RICE

SERVES 4, READY IN 20 MINUTES

2 tablespoons vegetable oil
1 brown onion, halved and cut
  into thin wedges
3 garlic cloves, finely chopped
400 g chicken thighs, thinly sliced
4 cups cooked rice
2 tablespoons fish sauce
1 tablespoon light soy sauce
¼ cup finely sliced spring onions
¼ cup roughly chopped fresh
  coriander
freshly ground black pepper
sliced cucumber to serve
lime wedges to serve

Omelette
3 eggs
1 teaspoon fish sauce
freshly ground black pepper
1 tablespoon vegetable oil

STEP 1
To make the omelette, whisk the eggs with the fish sauce, 1 tablespoon of water and a generous grinding of pepper.

STEP 2
Heat 1 tablespoon of vegetable oil in a wok over high heat. Pour in the eggs and use your spatula to push the egg mixture from the centre out to the edges. Once the egg is nearly set, flip it over and cook for another minute. Transfer the cooked egg to a chopping board and roughly slice.

STEP 3
Heat 2 tablespoons of vegetable oil in the same wok over high heat. Add the onion and garlic and cook for about a minute. Add the chicken and stir-fry for 4–5 minutes, until it is cooked. Now add your rice, the fish sauce and the soy sauce. Toss until the ingredients are well combined. Remove from the heat and toss through the spring onions, coriander and a generous grinding of pepper.

STEP 4
Serve with the cucumber and lime wedges.

NASI GORENG

SERVES 4, READY IN 20 MINUTES

4 tablespoons vegetable oil
4 eggs
1 brown onion, thinly sliced
3 garlic cloves, finely chopped
½ teaspoon shrimp paste*
200 g peeled and deveined raw
  prawns (about 400 g if you're
  buying unpeeled)
200 g pork fillet, thinly sliced
4 cups cooked rice
2 tablespoons light soy sauce
1 tablespoon fish sauce
1 teaspoon kecap manis*
¼ cup fried shallots*
1 Lebanese cucumber, sliced
sambal oelek* to serve

STEP 1
Heat half the vegetable oil in a wok or non-stick frying pan over high heat and fry the eggs in batches until cooked to your liking. Transfer the eggs to a plate and set aside until ready to serve.

STEP 2
Place the same wok back over high heat and pour in the remaining vegetable oil. When the oil is hot, add the onion and garlic and cook for about a minute. Add the shrimp paste and stir-fry for another minute, until the paste dissolves. Add the prawns and pork and stir-fry for 2–3 minutes, or until just cooked. Add the rice, soy sauce, fish sauce and kecap manis and toss for 2 minutes, or until well combined.

STEP 3
Pile onto serving plates and top with the cooked eggs and fried shallots. Serve with the cucumber and sambal oelek.

* Shrimp paste can be found in some major supermarkets or any Asian grocer.

* Kecap manis is an Indonesian sweet soy sauce, available in the Asian aisle of most major supermarkets or from an Asian grocer.

* Jars or packets of ready-made fried shallots or onions can be bought from the Asian aisle of most supermarkets or an Asian grocer.

* Sambal oelek is a spicy paste made from fresh red chillies and can be found in the Asian aisle of some supermarkets or at any Asian grocer.

SPICED INDIAN RICE

25 g butter
6 green cardamom pods,
   lightly crushed
1 cinnamon stick
1 teaspoon cumin seeds
2 cups basmati rice
4 cups chicken stock
¼ cup flaked almonds
3 tablespoons finely chopped
   fresh coriander

Caramelised onions
2 tablespoons vegetable oil
2 brown onions, halved and
   finely sliced

The buttery, spiced rice and sweet onion topping make this a super tasty addition to any Indian-inspired meal.

STEP 1

Heat the butter over medium–high heat in a deep saucepan. Add the cardamom, cinnamon stick and cumin seeds and fry for about a minute, until fragrant. Add the rice and chicken stock and stir to combine. Bring to the boil, cover with a lid and turn the heat to low. Simmer for 16 minutes until all the chicken stock has been absorbed by the rice. Remove from the heat and let the saucepan stand, covered, for 3 minutes.

STEP 2

While your rice is cooking, heat the vegetable oil in a frying pan over medium–high heat and cook the onions for 10–12 minutes, or until dark golden brown. Don't skimp on the cooking time here – you want your onions to be sticky and sweet.

STEP 3

Once your rice is done, spoon it onto a large platter. Serve it topped with the fried onions, almonds and fresh coriander.

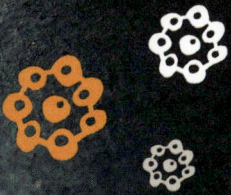

CONGEE

Chinese congee is generally a very thick, long-simmered rice soup flavoured with any number of different ingredients and toppings. My express versions are simmered relatively quickly so they have a much lighter soup consistency rather than the more traditional porridge texture.

A steaming bowl of congee is such a comforting dinner for me but can I let you in on a little secret? It works wonders as a breakfast hangover cure!

PORK & MUSHROOM CONGEE

SERVES 4, READY IN 30 MINUTES

1 cup long grain rice

3 cups chicken stock

4 cm piece ginger, peeled and finely julienned

2 tablespoons light soy sauce

¼ cup shaoxing (Chinese cooking wine)*

chilli flakes to serve

Topping

1 tablespoon vegetable oil

3 garlic cloves, roughly chopped

200 g pork mince

200 g mixed Asian mushrooms such as shiitake, oyster, shimeji, wood ear, roughly chopped

3 tablespoons light soy sauce

¼ cup finely sliced spring onions

STEP 1

Place the rice, stock, half the ginger, the soy sauce and the shaoxing in a saucepan over medium–high heat. Bring to the boil. Reduce the heat to medium and simmer, loosely covered, for 20 minutes, or until the rice is soft.

STEP 2

While your rice is cooking, make your pork and mushroom topping. Heat the vegetable oil in a wok over high heat. Add the garlic and pork and stir-fry for 2–3 minutes, or until the pork is just cooked. Add the mushrooms and soy sauce and stir-fry for another minute, until the mushrooms have softened. Remove from the heat and toss through the spring onions. Keep warm until your congee is ready.

STEP 3

Check the consistency of your congee. If it is too thick, add up to 1 cup of water and bring back to a simmer briefly. Divide the congee between the serving bowls. Top with the pork and mushroom mixture, the remaining ginger and the chilli flakes. Serve warm.

* Shaoxing is a Chinese wine made from fermented rice. Find it at your Asian grocer and some major supermarkets.

FISH CONGEE

SERVES 4, READY IN 30 MINUTES

1 cup long grain rice
4 cm piece ginger, peeled and
  finely julienned
2 tablespoons light soy sauce,
  plus 4 extra teaspoons to serve
¼ cup shaoxing (Chinese cooking
  wine)*
300 g snapper fillet, sliced into
  1 cm-wide strips
¼ cup finely sliced spring onions
¼ cup roughly chopped fresh
  coriander
4 teaspoons sesame oil
¼ cup fried shallots*
freshly ground black pepper

STEP 1

Place the rice, 3 cups of water, half the ginger, 2 tablespoons of the soy sauce and the shaoxing in a saucepan over medium–high heat. Bring to the boil. Reduce the heat to medium and simmer, loosely covered, for 20 minutes, or until the rice is soft.

STEP 2

Gently stir through the fish and simmer for a further 2 minutes, or until the fish is just cooked. Check the consistency of your congee. If it is too thick, add up to 1 cup of water and bring back to a simmer briefly. Divide the congee between the serving bowls. Top each serving with spring onions, coriander, the remaining ginger, a teaspoon of sesame oil, a teaspoon of soy sauce and crunchy fried shallots. Finish with a generous grinding of pepper. Serve warm.

CHICKEN & EGG CONGEE

SERVES 4, READY IN 30 MINUTES

1 cup long grain rice
2 chicken thighs, very thinly
  sliced
4 cm piece ginger, peeled and
  finely julienned
2 tablespoons light soy sauce,
  plus 8 extra teaspoons to serve
¼ cup shaoxing (Chinese cooking
  wine)*
2 eggs
¼ cup finely sliced spring onions
¼ cup roughly chopped fresh
  coriander
1 long red chilli, finely sliced
4 teaspoons Chinese black
  vinegar*
freshly ground black pepper

STEP 1

Place the rice, 3 cups of water, the chicken, half the ginger, 2 tablespoons of the soy sauce and the shaoxing in a saucepan over medium–high heat. Bring to the boil. Reduce the heat to medium and simmer, loosely covered, for 20 minutes, or until the rice is soft.

STEP 2

While your rice is cooking, place the eggs in a small saucepan and cover with water. Bring to a gentle simmer over medium–high heat. Simmer for 5 minutes. Remove, peel and slice in half. Set aside until ready to serve.

STEP 3

Check the consistency of your congee. If it is too thick, add up to 1 cup of water and bring back to a simmer briefly. Divide the congee between the serving bowls. Top each serving with an egg half, spring onions, coriander, chilli slices, the remaining ginger, 2 teaspoons of soy sauce and 1 teaspoon of vinegar. Season with pepper and serve warm.

* Shaoxing is a Chinese wine made from fermented rice. Find it at your Asian grocer and some major supermarkets.

* Chinese black vinegar is a dark, complex vinegar that you can find at your Asian grocer.

* Jars or packets of ready-made fried shallots or onions can be bought from the Asian aisle of most supermarkets or an Asian grocer.

SWEET THINGS & DRINKS

01. COCONUT—BANANA FRENCH TOAST — 192
02. KAFFIR LIME—STRAWBERRY TARTS — 194
03. MACADAMIA, MANGO & GINGER CUPS — 197
04. COCONUT—CARAMEL BANANA SUNDAE — 198
05. ALMOND & GINGER WONTON CRISPS — 200
06. LIME CURD — 203
07. WATERMELON, GINGER & MINT JUICE — 204
08. CHAI TEA — 206
09. GINGER, LEMONGRASS & HONEY TEA — 207
10. MANGO LASSI — 208

COCONUT–BANANA FRENCH TOAST

2 eggs

1 cup coconut milk

4 tablespoons brown sugar

½ teaspoon ground cinnamon

¼ teaspoon sea salt

4 thick slices brioche (white, sourdough or raisin bread are also good)

25 g unsalted butter

2 large bananas, cut into bite-sized chunks

maple syrup to serve

icing sugar to serve

lime wedges to serve

Breakfast, dessert or even dinner, I won't judge.

STEP 1

Whisk the eggs, coconut milk, brown sugar, cinnamon and sea salt together in a large shallow bowl.

STEP 2

Dip two slices of the brioche (or other bread) into the egg mixture. Give them a good squish around on both sides. Melt half the butter in a large non-stick frying pan over medium–high heat. Cook the eggy slices for 1–2 minutes on each side, or until golden brown. Transfer to a plate and keep warm. Repeat the process with the remaining two slices.

STEP 3

Arrange the French toast on serving plates, top with the banana slices and pour over lashings of maple syrup. Sift over a sprinkling of icing sugar and serve with lime wedges for a bit of last-minute tang.

KAFFIR LIME–STRAWBERRY TARTS

500 g strawberries, hulled
and quartered
2 tablespoons white sugar
2 kaffir lime leaves, stems
removed, very finely chopped
finely grated zest of 1 lime
2 tablespoons lime juice
200 g mascarpone
2 tablespoons icing sugar
18 small store-bought mini
sweet tart cases

Limes and strawberries make such a handsome couple. This effortless dessert or afternoon-tea treat is best assembled just before serving so that your pastry cases don't get too soggy.

STEP 1

In a large bowl, toss together the strawberries, sugar, kaffir lime leaves, lime zest and lime juice. Set aside for 5 minutes.

STEP 2

In a separate bowl, mix the mascarpone and icing sugar together until well combined.

STEP 3

Place a generous dollop of the mascarpone in each tart case and top with strawberries. You'll have a sweet, limey syrup in the bottom of your strawberry bowl. Spoon that tasty syrup over the strawberries and serve.

MACADAMIA, MANGO & GINGER CUPS

SERVES 6, READY IN 30 MINUTES

150 g sponge finger (savoiardi) biscuits (about 8 biscuits)

600 g ripe mango flesh (about 2 large peeled mangoes should do it), diced

80 g honey-roasted macadamias, roughly chopped (use plain unsalted macadamias as an alternative)

Honey–vanilla yoghurt

2 cups Greek-style natural yoghurt

2 tablespoons honey

1 vanilla pod, split and seeds scraped

Ginger syrup

½ cup white sugar

1 tablespoon finely grated fresh ginger

These little cups of tropical goodness are a wonderfully easy way to finish a dinner party. If you're making them in advance, assemble the biscuits, mango and honey–vanilla yoghurt in your glasses and pop them in the fridge. To serve, all you need to do is sprinkle the tops with those crunchy macadamias.

STEP 1

To make the honey–vanilla yoghurt, combine the yoghurt, honey and vanilla seeds in a large bowl. Set aside in the fridge until ready to assemble.

STEP 2

To make the ginger syrup, place the sugar, ginger and 1 cup of water in a small saucepan and simmer over high heat for 2 minutes, or until the sugar dissolves and forms a light syrup. Remove from the heat and set aside.

STEP 3

In the meantime, break each sponge finger biscuit into three roughly even pieces.

STEP 4

Place six 125 ml glasses or ramekins on your kitchen bench. Place a layer of sponge finger biscuit pieces into the bottom of each glass. Spoon over 2–3 tablespoons of the warm ginger syrup to soften the biscuits. Top with a couple of spoonfuls of mango, then a good dollop of the honey–vanilla yoghurt.

STEP 5

Place in the fridge to chill until ready to serve. Sprinkle with honey-roasted macadamias and serve.

COCONUT–CARAMEL BANANA SUNDAE

½ cup dried coconut flakes
4 bananas, peeled and cut into
  small chunks
8 scoops vanilla ice cream
2 honeycomb chocolate bars
  such as Violet Crumble or
  Crunchie bars, roughly chopped
½ cup pecans, roughly chopped

Coconut caramel
100 g butter
1 cup brown sugar
½ cup coconut cream
½ teaspoon sea salt

In my mind, a good sundae has a creamy ice cream base, an element of crunch and a sweet, oozing sauce. Strawberries, raspberries or mango work just as well as the banana in this recipe.

STEP 1
To make the coconut caramel, place the butter, brown sugar, coconut cream and salt in a small saucepan over medium–high heat. Whisk the mixture together as the butter melts. When the mixture is smooth, simmer for 3–4 minutes, until the caramel coats the back of a wooden spoon. Remove from the heat.

STEP 2
Toast the coconut flakes in a dry frying pan over high heat for 2–3 minutes, or until golden. Set aside until ready to serve.

STEP 3
Divide the bananas between the serving bowls and top with ice cream and generous spoonfuls of coconut caramel. Sprinkle with honeycomb chocolate, pecans and toasted coconut flakes.

ALMOND & GINGER WONTON CRISPS

MAKES 25, READY IN 30 MINUTES

1 egg white
2 tablespoons honey
1 cup flaked almonds
¼ cup caster sugar
1 teaspoon ground ginger
25 wonton wrappers

These crispy little wafers are ridiculously addictive. Just the right amount of gingery spice and sweet, nutty crunch. Serve with coffee, tea or as a lunchbox snack.

STEP 1
Preheat the oven to 200°C. Line two large oven trays with baking paper.

STEP 2
Lightly whisk the egg white and honey in a small bowl until just combined. Set aside for later.

STEP 3
Place the almonds in a plastic bag and use a rolling pin or the base of a heavy pan to crush them up a little.

STEP 4
Place the crushed almonds, caster sugar and ginger in a bowl and toss to combine.

STEP 5
Lay the wonton wrappers on the lined baking trays and brush the top of each wrapper with the egg white mixture. Top with liberal sprinklings of the crushed almonds. Place the trays in the preheated oven and bake for 7–8 minutes, or until golden brown and crisp. Transfer to a cake rack to cool.

LIME CURD

100 g unsalted butter,
  roughly chopped
1 cup caster sugar
1 tablespoon finely grated
  lime zest
½ cup lime juice, strained
4 kaffir lime leaves, stems
  removed, finely sliced
3 eggs, lightly whisked

Ooooh, this stuff is devilishly good. It keeps for up to a month in the fridge and has so many tasty uses. You can make lime tarts by filling store-bought sweet pastry tarts with the curd. Or spread it between layers of sponge cake along with some whipped cream. But my ultimate weeknight dessert involves an extra-large scoop of vanilla ice cream topped with an extra-large spoonful of tangy lime curd.

STEP 1
Place the butter, sugar, lime zest, lime juice and kaffir lime leaves in a saucepan over medium–low heat for 3–4 minutes, or until the sugar dissolves. Remove from the heat, pour into a large bowl and cool for 1 minute.

STEP 2
Whisk the eggs into the butter mixture. Strain into a clean, heavy-based saucepan and place over medium–low heat. Cook, stirring, for 12 minutes, or until the mixture coats the back of a wooden spoon. It will thicken further as it cools.

STEP 3
Spoon the hot curd into sterilised jars and seal. Store in the fridge for up to 4 weeks.

WATERMELON, GINGER & MINT JUICE

SERVES 4, READY IN 10 MINUTES

1 kg peeled watermelon,
  chopped
1 tablespoon finely grated
  fresh ginger
¼ cup mint leaves
2 tablespoons lime juice
1 heaped cup ice cubes

I love a pink drink. This makes a refreshing breakfast juice or add a splash of vodka for an evening cocktail.

STEP 1
Place the watermelon, ginger, mint, lime juice and ice in a blender and whizz until smooth.

STEP 2
Pour into glasses and serve straight away.

CHAI TEA

2 cups milk
4 green cardamom pods,
  lightly crushed
2 cinnamon sticks
1 teaspoon fennel seeds
4 cm piece ginger, peeled
  and finely sliced
4 tea bags

You can serve this beautifully spiced tea hot, or chill it and add ice cubes for a cool summer drink.

STEP 1
In a saucepan over medium–high heat, bring the milk, cardamom, cinnamon sticks, fennel seeds, ginger and 2 cups of water to a gentle simmer.

STEP 2
Wrap the tea bag strings around a wooden spoon. When the milk mixture is simmering, place the tea bags in it, resting the spoon on the rim of the saucepan so that the tea bags dangle in the milk. Simmer for 1 minute, then remove the pan from the heat and let the tea steep for 2–3 minutes.

STEP 3
Remove the tea bags and pour the tea through a strainer into cups.

GINGER, LEMONGRASS & HONEY TEA

SERVES 6, READY IN 15 MINUTES

10 cm piece ginger, peeled and thinly sliced

2 lemongrass stalks (white part only), bruised and cut into 4 cm batons

¼ cup honey (use more or less depending on how sweet you like it)

Tissue box – check. Chicken soup – check. Couch – check. Ginger, lemongrass and honey tea – check. My ultimate sniffly nose checklist.

STEP 1
Place all the ingredients in a saucepan with 4 cups of water. Heat over high heat until boiling then reduce the heat to medium and simmer for 5 minutes. Remove from the heat and let the tea steep for 2–3 minutes.

STEP 2
Pour the tea through a strainer into tea cups.

MANGO LASSI

600 g ripe mango flesh (about
  2 large peeled mangoes should
  do it), roughly chopped
1 cup natural yoghurt
½ cup milk
2 tablespoons honey
2 heaped cups ice cubes

Frozen mango works a treat in this recipe but you could also use fresh or frozen berries. Use more or less milk to make your lassi thicker or thinner to taste.

STEP 1
Place all the ingredients in a blender and whizz until smooth. (Do this in batches if your blender is too small.)

STEP 2
Pour into large glasses and serve immediately.

WEEKLY DINNER PLANNER

Here's some inspiration for how you might like to use your *Asia Express* recipes from Monday through to Friday. And I've included my 'Express tips' on how to make those weeknight dinners even easier. Happy cooking!

MONDAY

Hainanese Chicken Rice (p.64)

Express tip: make a double batch of the poached chicken. Use half of the chicken tonight and save the rest for tomorrow's dinner.

TUESDAY

Miso Chicken Noodle Soup (p.66)

WEDNESDAY

Thai Green Seafood Curry (p.50)

Express tip: make 8 cups of cooked rice. Serve half with your curry and save the rest for tomorrow's dinner.

THURSDAY

Nasi Goreng (p.182)

FRIDAY

Asian Pork Burgers (p.106)

MONDAY

Coconut–Pumpkin Soup (p.164)

Express tip: make a double batch and freeze any leftovers in single-serve containers to take as work lunches this week.

TUESDAY

Sichuan Pork & Green Beans (p.116)

WEDNESDAY

Duck Red Curry Noodle Soup (p.93)

Express tip: cook a double batch of the duck breasts. Use half of the duck tonight and the rest can be saved and sliced cold for tomorrow's salad.

THURSDAY

Duck Noodle Salad (p.88)

FRIDAY

Korean Steak Sandwich (p.126)

MONDAY

Thai Chicken & Ginger Stir-fry (p.87)

TUESDAY

Char Siu Pork (p.96)

Express tip: make a double batch. For tonight, serve with rice, cucumber and perhaps Wok-fried Asian greens (page 174). Save leftover pork for tomorrow's dinner.

WEDNESDAY

Char Siu Pork Noodle Soup (p.118)

THURSDAY

Roast Pepper Beef with Ponzu (p.131)

Express tip: make a double batch of the ponzu and save some for tomorrow's dinner.

FRIDAY

Sesame Tuna with Ponzu (p.31)

COOKING FOR FRIENDS

Cooking for family and friends doesn't have to mean hours on end in the kitchen. I've put together some of my favourite express party menus from the recipes in this book along with a few of my planning tips. Enjoy!

EXPRESS DINNER PARTY FOR 4

Dinner parties are all about friend time … not kitchen time. You can make your pumpkin soup days or even weeks in advance (simply freeze and reheat if you prefer). Your miso butter will keep in the freezer; just take it out an hour or so before you cook your steaks. Toss together your Red Potato Salad before guests arrive. And have all your sundae ingredients made up and ready to assemble at the last minute. Now all you need is about 10 minutes in the kitchen to cook your steaks and a few minutes to scoop and serve your sundaes … perfect!

....

>>> Coconut–Pumpkin Soup (p.164)
>>> Steak with Miso Butter (p.124)
>>> Red Potato Salad (p.168)
>>> Coconut–Caramel Banana Sundae (p.198)

EASY–PEASY LUNCH FOR 8

Serving a whole side of salmon is such an easy way to please a crowd. Pop your Spiced Roasted Salmon in the oven 20 minutes before you want to eat. The Masala Chickpeas & Spinach can be made in advance and simply reheated to serve. Make your Spiced Indian Rice before your guests arrive and cover it with foil to keep warm. My friends are always hungry so I like to make a double batch of the Indian Lamb Kofta to serve as a starter for this number of people. Pop your kofta into the oven just before your guests arrive. And have your Kaffir Lime Strawberry Tart components made up and ready to assemble when you please.

....

>>> Indian Lamb Kofta (p.142)
>>> Spiced Roasted Salmon (p.26)
>>> Spiced Indian Rice (p.184)
>>> Masala Chickpeas & Spinach (p.165)
>>> Kaffir Lime–Strawberry Tarts (p.194)

THAI FEAST FOR 6

I love the theatre of seeing prawn cakes puff up and turn golden in bubbling oil. So grab a glass of wine and a friend and make these when your guests arrive so they're served piping hot. You can make your Panang Chicken Curry in advance and reheat it when the time comes. Cook your Wok-fried Asian Greens just before your guests arrive and cover with foil to keep warm. Have your Thai Grilled Pork Salad ingredients prepared and ready to toss together, but cook and slice your pork scotch steaks at the last minute so that the pork is warm when you assemble the salad. Keep your Macadamia, Mango & Ginger Cups in the fridge and simply top with the crunchy macadamia nuts when you're ready to serve.

....

Prawn Cakes with Chilli–Lime Sauce (p.18)

Panang Chicken Curry (p.69)

Thai Grilled Pork Salad (p.105)

Wok-fried Asian Greens (p.174)

Steamed Jasmine Rice (p.178)

Macadamia, Mango & Ginger Cups (p.197)

INDIAN CURRY NIGHT FOR 6

I adore the fragrant scent of spices that fills my kitchen when I make this Indian spread for my friends. The vegetable curry can be made in advance and reheated to serve. Make up your peshwari naan beforehand but pop them in the oven 5 minutes before serving. For the South Indian Fish Curry, you can simmer the sauce up to Step 1, but add the coconut milk and fish 5 minutes before you sit down to eat. The Bombay Potatoes and Spiced Indian Rice can be made in advance and reheated. And those moreish Almond & Ginger Wonton Crisps can be baked in the afternoon. The Mango Lassi and Chai Tea are best made just before serving. Make a double batch of the lassi and tea to make sure there's enough to go around.

....

Mango Lassi (p.208)

South Indian Fish Curry (p.53)

Vegetable Curry with Peshwari Naan (p.154)

Bombay Potatoes (p.161)

Spiced Indian Rice (p.184)

Chai Tea (p.206)

Almond & Ginger Wonton Crisps (p.200)

ASIAN BANQUET FOR 6

I love the spectacle of a table laden with dishes ready to share and pass around. You can cook the Korean Seafood Pancakes before guests arrive and have them warming in the oven. For the Duck with Hoisin Plum Sauce, you can sear the duck breasts in advance and pre-make your sauce. Then just pop your duck in the oven to finish cooking about 10 minutes before you want to eat. The Chilli Eggplant and Chinese Sausage & Egg Fried Rice will keep warm under foil, but you'll need to wok-fry your Vietnamese Shaking Beef just before serving. Make your Lime Curd well in advance and store it in the fridge, then all you'll need to do is spoon it over scoops of creamy vanilla ice cream to serve.

»» Korean Seafood Pancakes (p.46)
»» Duck with Hoisin Plum Sauce (p.90)
»» Vietnamese Shaking Beef (p.137)
»» Chilli Eggplant (p.173)
»» Chinese Sausage & Egg Fried Rice (p.181)
»» Lime Curd with Vanilla Ice Cream (p.203)

THANKS

These pages would not be possible without the unwavering support of a great many special people.

Mary Small – you are impossibly amazing. Your friendship and belief in me from the very beginning means the world to me. Thank you a hundred times over.

Big love to the 'A-team'. Thank you John Laurie for your awesome pictures and valuable cricket commentary. To Tom Friml for photographic assistance and for eating all my food with such gusto. To Deb Kaloper for being the beautiful person that you are and for your impeccable taste in styling. To Emma Christian and Emma Warren for your tireless work in the kitchen. To Hannah Marshall for your makeup magic. Thank you to the super talented Jane Winning and Clare Marshall for making this whole book come together so beautifully.

A huge thankyou to Mark and Melinda Haldane for sharing your beautiful house and kitchen. And thank you Lily for keeping us company.

Thank you for your brilliant design work Michelle Mackintosh. And thank you Jean Kingett for your eagle-eyed editing.

To my mum and dad for being the best parents a girl could wish for. Thank you Mum for being my kitchen hand, sous chef and head chef. Thank you Dad for being my most trusted and brutally honest taste tester.

And to my darling husband Tim – thank you for believing in me, putting up with me and for being my best friend always.

INDEX

A

Almond & ginger wonton crisps 200
Asian greens
  Wok-fried Asian greens 175
Asian pork burgers 106
Asian vegetable omelette 170

B

bamboo shoots 11
bananas
  Coconut–banana French toast 192
  Coconut–caramel banana sundae 198
Barbecued chicken banh mi 60
beans
  Sichuan pork & green beans 116
beef
  Beef pho 132
  Korean steak sandwich 126
  Roast pepper beef with ponzu 131
  Sichuan pepper beef noodles 138
  Soy–ginger eye fillet steaks 128
  Spicy cumin beef 140
  Steak with miso butter 124
  Thai beef salad 134
  Vietnamese beef noodle salad 129
  Vietnamese shaking beef 137
Bombay potatoes 161
burgers, *see* sandwiches/burgers
Burmese prawn curry 41

C

cabbage
  Red potato salad 168
  Sweet chilli–coconut coleslaw 167
Chai tea 206
Char siu pork 96
Char siu pork noodle soup 118
chicken
  Barbecued chicken banh mi 60
  Basic poached chicken 62–3
  Chicken & egg congee 188
  Chicken & egg donburi 82
  Chicken karaage 84
  Garam masala chicken 77
  Hainanese chicken rice 64
  Hot & sour chicken soup 81
  Hot 'n' spicy chicken wings 72
  Korean grilled chicken 79
  Miso chicken noodle soup 66
  Mum's sweet & sour chicken 75
  Panang chicken curry 69
  Rendang chicken wings 72
  Tandoori chicken wings 71
  Thai chicken & ginger stir-fry 87
  Thai chicken fried rice 182
  Vietnamese chicken salad 58
  Vietnamese lemongrass chicken 80

chickpeas
  Masala chickpeas & spinach 165
chillies 140
  Chilli eggplant 173
  Chilli mayo 106
  Chilli sambal 20
  Chilli sauce 162
  Chilli vinegar 103
  Korean chilli paste 12
  sambal oelek 13
  sriracha chilli sauce 13
  Sriracha egg & ham cups 110
  Sweet chilli–coconut coleslaw 167
  Sweet chilli & lime (fish) parcels 33
Chinese black vinegar 11
Chinese sausage & egg fried rice 181
coconut
  Coconut–pumpkin soup 164
  Coconut–banana French toast 192
  Coconut–caramel banana sundae 198
  Sweet chilli–coconut coleslaw 167
congee
  Chicken & egg congee 188
  Fish congee 188
  Pork & mushroom congee 187
Coriander & garlic (fish) parcels 34
crab
  Crab omelette 36
  Thai yellow curry crab 45
Crab omelette 36
Crispy egg tofu 162
Crispy fish with chilli sambal 20
Crumbed coriander fish fingers 42
curry 69
  Burmese prawn curry 41
  Curry-spiced corn fritters 150
  Duck red curry noodle soup 93
  Panang chicken curry 69
  South Indian fish curry 53
  Thai green seafood curry 50
  Thai red curry–poached salmon 40
  Thai yellow curry crab 45
  Vegetable curry with peshwari naan 154
Curry-spiced corn fritters 150

D

Dan dan noodles 102
desserts *see* sweets
drinks
  Chai tea 206
  Ginger, lemongrass & honey tea 207
  Mango lassi 208
  Watermelon, ginger & mint juice 204
duck
  Duck with hoisin plum sauce 90
  Duck noodle salad 88
  Duck red curry noodle soup 93

E

eggplant
Chilli eggplant 173
Pork & eggplant stir-fry 115
eggs
Asian vegetable omelette 170
Chicken & egg congee 188
Chicken & egg donburi 82
Chinese sausage & egg fried rice 181
Fried eggs with crazy sauce 156
Nasi goreng 182
Sriracha egg & ham cups 110
Vietnamese pork & egg rice 109

F

fish
Coriander & garlic (fish) parcels 34
Crispy fish with chilli sambal 20
Crumbed coriander fish fingers 42
Fish congee 188
fish sauce 11
Sesame tuna with ponzu 31
Slightly charry char siu salmon 54
South Indian fish curry 53
Soy & ginger (fish) parcels 34
Spiced roasted salmon 26
Sweet chilli & lime (fish) parcels 33
Thai red curry–poached salmon 40
Vietnamese turmeric & dill fish 24
see also seafood
Five-spice lamb cutlets 141
Fried eggs with crazy sauce 156
fried rice
Chinese sausage & egg fried rice 181
Nasi goreng 182
Thai chicken fried rice 182

G

garam masala 11
Garam masala chicken 77
ginger 87
Almond & ginger wonton crisps 200
Ginger, lemongrass & honey tea 207
Macadamia, mango & ginger cups 197
Soy–ginger eye fillet steaks 128
Soy & ginger (fish) parcels 34
Spring onion & ginger sauce 64
Thai chicken & ginger stir-fry 87
Watermelon, ginger & mint juice 204
gochujang (Korean chilli paste) 12

H

Hainanese chicken rice 64
Hoisin glaze 141
Honey–vanilla yoghurt 197
Hot & sour chicken soup 81
Hot 'n' spicy chicken wings 72

I

Indian lamb kofta 142

K

Kaffir lime–strawberry tarts 194
'Kewpie' (Japanese) mayonnaise 12
Korean chilli paste 12
Korean grilled chicken 79
Korean seafood pancakes 46
Korean steak sandwich 126

L

lamb
Five-spice lamb cutlets 141
Indian lamb kofta 142
Spicy lamb rack 145
Tandoori lamb cutlets 146
Lime curd 203
Lobster
Grilled lobster with kaffir lime butter 39

M

Macadamia, mango & ginger cups 197
Mango lassi 208
Masala chickpeas & spinach 165
mayonnaise
Chilli mayo 106
'Kewpie' (Japanese) 12
Mint & coriander yoghurt 26
Mint yoghurt 145
miso
Miso butter 124
Miso chicken noodle soup 66
Miso mushroom spaghetti 158
shiro miso 13
Mum's sweet & sour chicken 75
mushrooms
Miso mushroom spaghetti 158
Pork & mushroom congee 187
Thai mushroom salad 153

N

Nasi goreng 182
noodles
Beef pho 132
Char siu pork noodle soup 118
Dan dan noodles 102
Duck noodle salad 88
Duck red curry noodle soup 93
Miso chicken noodle soup 66
Pork & prawn hokkien mee 100
Sichuan pepper beef noodles 138
Sticky pork noodle salad 112
Thai pork noodles in gravy 103
Vietnamese beef noodle salad 129

O

omelette, Asian vegetable 170
onions
  Caramelised onions 184
  fried onions 11
  Spring onion & ginger sauce 64
oyster sauce 12

P

palm sugar 12
Panang chicken curry 69
panko breadcrumbs 12
pasta
  Miso mushroom spaghetti 158
Peshwari naan 154
Pomegranate raita 146
pork
  Asian pork burgers 106
  Char siu pork 96
  Char siu pork noodle soup 118
  Nasi goreng 182
  Pork & eggplant stir-fry 115
  Pork & mushroom congee 187
  Pork & prawn hokkien mee 100
  Sichuan pork & green beans 116
  Spicy Korean pork 120
  Sriracha egg & ham cups 110
  Sticky pork noodle salad 112
  Thai grilled pork salad 105
  Tonkatsu 98
  Vietnamese pork & egg rice 109
potatoes
  Bombay potatoes 161
  Red potato salad 168
prawns
  Burmese prawn curry 41
  Nasi goreng 182
  Pork & prawn hokkien mee 100
  Prawn cakes with chilli–lime sauce 18
  Prawn char kway teow 28
  Prawn mee goreng 51
  Vietnamese prawn salad 48
  Wok-fried prawns 23

R

Red potato salad 168
Rendang chicken wings 72
rice
  Chicken & egg congee 188
  Chicken & egg donburi 82
  Chinese sausage & egg fried rice 181
  Fish congee 188
  Hainanese chicken rice 64
  Nasi goreng 182
  Pork & mushroom congee 187
  Spiced Indian rice 184
  Steamed jasmine rice 178–9

Thai chicken fried rice 182
Vietnamese pork & egg rice 109
Roast pepper beef with ponzu 131

S

salads
  Duck noodle salad 88
  Red potato salad 168
  Sticky pork noodle salad 112
  Thai beef salad 134
  Thai grilled pork salad 105
  Thai mushroom salad 153
  Vietnamese beef noodle salad 129
  Vietnamese chicken salad 58
  Vietnamese prawn salad 48
sambal oelek 13
sandwiches/burgers
  Asian pork burgers 106
  Barbecued chicken banh mi 60
  Korean steak sandwich 126
sauces
  Chilli sauce 162
  Chilli–lime sauce 18
  fish sauce 11
  oyster sauce 12
  Ponzu 31, 131
  soy sauce 14
  Spiced yoghurt sauce 142
  Spicy dipping sauce 46
  Spring onion and ginger sauce 64
  sriracha chilli sauce 13
  Tartare sauce 42
  tonkatsu sauce 14
sausage
  Chinese sausage & egg fried rice 181
seafood
  Coriander & garlic (fish) parcels 34
  Crab omelette 36
  Crispy fish with chilli sambal 20
  Crumbed coriander fish fingers 42
  Fish congee 188
  Grilled lobster with kaffir lime butter 39
  Korean seafood pancakes 46
  Sesame tuna with ponzu 31
  Slightly charry char siu salmon 54
  South Indian fish curry 53
  Soy & ginger (fish) parcels 34
  Spiced roasted salmon 26
  Sweet chilli & lime fish parcels 33
  Thai green seafood curry 50
  Thai red curry–poached salmon 40
  Thai yellow curry crab 45
  Vietnamese turmeric & dill fish 24
sesame oil 13
Sesame tuna with ponzu 31
shallots, fried 11
shaoxing wine 13

shichimi togarashi 13
shiro miso 13
shrimp, dried 11
shrimp paste 14
Sichuan pepper beef noodles 138
Sichuan peppercorns 14
Sichuan pork & green beans 116
Slightly charry char siu salmon 54
soup
  Beef pho 132
  Char siu pork noodle soup 118
  Coconut–pumpkin soup 164
  Duck red curry noodle soup 93
  Hot & sour chicken soup 81
  Miso chicken noodle soup 66
South Indian fish curry 53
Soy–ginger eye fillet steaks 128
Soy & ginger (fish) parcels 34
soy sauce 14
Spiced Indian rice 184
Spiced roasted salmon 26
Spicy cumin beef 140
Spicy Korean pork 120
Spicy lamb rack 145
spinach
  Masala chickpeas & spinach 165
Spring onion & ginger sauce 64
sriracha chilli sauce 13
Sriracha egg & ham cups 110
Steak with miso butter 124
Steamed jasmine rice 178–9
Sticky pork noodle salad 112
stir-fries
  Pork & eggplant stir-fry 115
  Thai chicken & ginger stir-fry 87
Sweet chilli–coconut coleslaw 167
Sweet chilli & lime (fish) parcels 33
sweets
  Coconut–banana French toast 192
  Coconut–caramel banana sundae 198
  Kaffir lime strawberry tarts 194
  Lime curd 203
  Macadamia, mango & ginger cups 197

T
Tandoori chicken wings 71
Tandoori lamb cutlets 146
Tartare sauce 42
Thai beef salad 134
Thai chicken & ginger stir-fry 87
Thai chicken fried rice 182
Thai green seafood curry 50
Thai grilled pork salad 105
Thai mushroom salad 153
Thai pork noodles in gravy 103
Thai red curry–poached salmon 40
Thai yellow curry crab 45

tofu
  Crispy egg tofu 162
Tonkatsu 98
tonkatsu sauce 14

V
vegetables
  Asian vegetable omelette 170
  Bombay potatoes 160
  Chilli eggplant 172
  Coconut–pumpkin soup 164
  Curry-spiced corn fritters 150
  Masala chickpeas & spinach 165
  Miso mushroom spaghetti 158
  Red potato salad 168
  Sweet chilli–coconut coleslaw 166
  Thai mushroom salad 152
  Vegetable curry with peshwari naan 154
  Wok-fried Asian greens 174
Vietnamese beef noodle salad 129
Vietnamese chicken salad 58
Vietnamese lemongrass chicken 80
Vietnamese pork & egg rice 109
Vietnamese prawn salad 48
Vietnamese shaking beef 137
Vietnamese turmeric & dill fish 24
vinegar
  Chilli vinegar 103
  Chinese black vinegar 11

W
Watermelon, ginger & mint juice 204
Wok-fried Asian greens 175
Wok-fried prawns 23
woks 15

Y
yoghurt
  Honey–vanilla yoghurt 197
  Mango lassi 208
  Mint & coriander yoghurt 26
  Mint yoghurt 145
  Pomegranate raita 146
  Spiced yoghurt sauce 142

A Plum book
First published in 2014 by
Pan Macmillan Australia Pty Limited
Level 25, 1 Market Street,
Sydney, NSW 2000, Australia

Level 1, 15–19 Claremont Street,
South Yarra, Victoria 3141, Australia

Text copyright © Marion Grasby 2014

Photographs copyright © John Laurie
2014, except images on the following
pages: 9, 216 © Sharyn Cairns

The moral right of the author has been
asserted.

Design by Michelle Mackintosh
Edited by Jean Kingett
Index by Jo Rudd
Photography by John Laurie
Prop and food styling by Deborah Kaloper
Food preparation by Emma Christian,
Marion Grasby and Emma Warren
Typeset by Pauline Haas
Colour reproduction by Splitting Image
Colour Studio

Printed and bound in China by
1010 Printing International Limited

A CIP catalogue record for this book is
available from the National Library of
Australia.

The publisher would like to thank the
following for their generosity in providing
props for the book: Craft Victoria and
Hamish and Grace.

10 9 8 7 6 5 4 3 2